Fragrant Intercession for Revival

Golden Bowls of Incense

Published 2009 by

IGNITE

Revival Network
An Ignite Revival Network Resource

©2009 Andrew Baguley

Ignite Prayer Book

CONTENTS

From the author

Forward

Introduction

Acknowledgements

Golden Bowls of Incense

Chapter 1 A New Song - The Church

Chapter 2 Perseverance pays off: Elijah

Chapter 3 Strong men lay hold of the Kingdom: Hezekiah

Chapter 4 Called to action: Nehemiah

Chapter 5 Can a nation be saved?: Abraham

Chapter 6 I will go: Ananias

Chapter 7 We'll walk the land: Joshua

Glimpses of Glory

Chapter 8 Memorials to God: Cornelius

Chapter 9 Revive your works, O Lord: Habakkuk

Chapter 10 It's worth groaning for!

Conclusion

Appendices

Useful Books and resources

Bibliography

FROM THE AUTHOR

Many excellent books have been written on the subject of prayer. These have helped Christians over the years to understand more about the theology of prayer and to develop their practice of prayer. We bear witness to the same experience in our Christian walk and to the countless thousands of saints who have prayed more than we shall ever know, for us, our salvation, our calling and the support we and our families need throughout our ministries, not to mention the powerful intercession for the Church and the nations of the world.

This book does not seek to compete with or replace any of those that have gone before. The Biblical call to faith in Christ is implicitly one which calls us to be a praying people. Text after text reinforces the truth that our relationship with God through Jesus Christ grows only by the witness of the Holy Spirit within us. The Holy Spirit can do no other than to do through us what Christ did, amongst which, is that continuous communion of prayer with the Father. It is this relationship which builds us in the likeness of Christ both in nature and power. This incarnation of Christ reveals a glorious bride to whom the world is attracted and through whom the world comes to hear about and believe in Christ.

We are filled with an urgency to see this happen in our time. We see the signs of this around the world and we pray for the renewal of the Methodist Church to her apostolic witness and evangelical fire in such a way that there will be revival in our land. We were excited and moved by the call to the United Methodist Church in America to pray for revival during the 1990s. We have witnessed for ourselves something of the fruit of this. We are thrilled too, to see the call to prayer repeatedly made in the Alpha Course and in the preparation for each Alpha Initiative. Hundreds and thousands of Christians across the denominations are gathering together to pray and God is hearing their cry. The astounding growth of new churches, like the Sunderland Christian Centre, Abundant Life in Bradford, Kings Church, NFI or Holy Trinity, Brompton with its numerous 'church plants' have their origins in the persistent Methodist prayer cry from the heart of its leaders and their intercessors. So too with the work of The Central Hall Westminster, Westminster Chapel and the Pioneer Churches to name but a few others. One of the fruits of this is a new ministry of 24 /7 intercessory prayer houses, the boiler house movement and the beacon prayer houses, like the one in Sandyford, Stoke-on-Trent. Many of these are part of a new war of the spirit in the UK Methodists. What God has and is still doing in Sunderland and Tyneside, Stoke-on-Trent and London He can and will surely do for elsewhere in the U.K. and in a largely non-Christian Europe. We have been deeply moved too by the Christian churches overseas that have been led to intercede for the UK. We shall never know this side of heaven how many intercessors God has spoken to about our need of prayer, but Brazilian, Argentinean, Peruvian, Kenyan and South Africans have been on their knees before God for our nation as we moved into the New Millennium. These are extraordinary times, but then our God is extraordinary and all things are possible for those who believe (Mark 9:23).

"A revival among believers is the great need of our day", wrote Andrew Murray in 'The Coming Christ' in 1989." And he added ", "A revived church is the only hope of a dying world".

I believe that we have moved on to the urgent need of our day, which is to pray for our nation to be saved. God is, I believe, shaking the governments and institutions in the so-called Christian west, at the beginning of the 21st century. Huge cracks have been exposed of godlessness, hypocrisy, greed, deceit, and wickedness. Ordinary people like us are now spied on, monitored, controlled and regulated in our work and private lives. Personal issues over responsibility have been sacrificed on the altars of "human rights" and "political correctness". The dark clouds of the end times are over us, but rather than defeat, this is perhaps the greatest moment for the Church of Christ. It may seem dark all around but it is impossible to lose your footing while on your knees.

When I was minister of a church espousing revival and the like in the mid 1990s I was struck by a quotation from the Scottish evangelist, Robert Murray McCheyne who said "What a man is on his knees before God, that he is, and nothing else".

Purpose of Book

The purpose of this book is threefold, namely:-
To inspire more fervent intercession for our nation.
To aid intercessory teams and house groups to understand the biblical warrant for Christians.
To encourage all of us to pray without ceasing.

May this book encourage and inspire us in all parts of the Church to call on the Lord while he is near, and in the words of a dear friend and intercessor move from "Polite to Power prayer' for the glory of God and the revival of this nation.

Andrew Baguley May 2009

FORWARD

By William Porter

I am delighted that Andrew has found the time to distil the lessons about prayer which God has been teaching him. They are lessons learned through the thrills and challenges involved in the journey of Christian leadership and pursuing God's presence.

What I believe is important about this book is that it concerns (i) revelatory praying, (ii) biblical praying and (iii) revival praying.(i) We are encouraged in scripture to ask for the Spirit of wisdom and revelation so that we might know God better. Andrew's teaching has the hallmark of both. God has shown him truth about effective prayer that has become bright and burning for him as he shares it. God has also allowed him to search out wisdom to help the church know how to press into spiritual breakthrough and transformation in our nation.(ii) There is a battle over our nation and the nations of the world. We are called to fight and act and pray as fully equipped Christians. The word of God and prayer help to equip us. Praying the word, as in anchoring our prayers on biblical truth about God and our relationship with him, is our most powerful weapon of warfare. This book opens our spiritual eyes to such a dimension of praying.(iii) Prayer must be linked to vision in order to be most effective. The vision of revival and outpourings of the Spirit run throughout this book. Andrew has had his own glimpses of glory and we are friends and fellow God-chasers on the journey of pursuing all He has in store for us in this generation of church. Andrew is a man who always inspires me by his spiritual hunger and faith in the Lord.

May you be blessed, equipped and inspired as you read.

William Porter

The Rev. Dr William Porter BA, MA, PhD is a Methodist Minister. He is leading a House of Prayer ministry and Fresh Expression of Church in Stoke on Trent, England. He is also the co-ordinator of Ignite Revival Network. He has written "A Fresh Look at Revivals and outpourings of The Spirit" and edited "Igniting Leadership" both published by Grove Books.

Introduction:

The gospels of Matthew and Luke record the teaching of Jesus on prayer (Matt. 6:9-13 & Luke 11: 1-11). It is easy for us to concentrate on the Lord's response to the question "Lord, teach us to pray, just as John taught his disciples" by looking only to the Lord's Prayer as our model. In Luke's gospel, Jesus goes on to expand the teaching in order to show the spiritual principles behind prayer. There are three principals. The first is **'persistence pays '***(vv5-8);* the second is **'God answers prayer'** (vv9-12); the third is **'the best prayer is to ask for the gift of the Spirit'** (v13). [Look at this in the context of passages such as Ephesians 5:18, John 16:8-15; 1 Cor. 2: 1-16; Romans *5:5* and 8:1-17] This gift of God's empowering presence within us enables us to "*pray in the Spirit on all occasions with all kinds of prayers and requests"* Ephesians 6:18) asking for what no eye has seen, no ear has heard and no mind has conceived about the promises for God's people, because we now know due to revelation(1 Cor. 2:10)

The Father answers when his children pray. In Luke 11:9 & 10 Jesus enumerates the prayers which are answered. They are asking prayers, seeking prayers and loud persistent prayers. This is because prayer is the heartbeat of a relationship between the Father and his children. He has opened up the way to him through Jesus, who Himself is The Way, The Truth and The life (John 14:6) and in whose Name we may ask all things.

Jesus made it clear that when we are in a fruitful relationship with God, which he compares to the vine and its grape bearing branches (John 15), then the Father will give us whatever we ask for in Jesus name (John 15:16).

In Matthews gospel we hear Jesus enumerate three principles behind persistent prayer. These are **asking, seeking and knocking.**

The asking prayer is a constant plea for help and favour from an extraordinarily generous Father who delights to give good gifts to his children. It is also a pleading on behalf of others (like the man in Luke 11:5-8) who cannot or will not ask for themselves. It is the basis of mission and pastoral care. It is Gethsemane praying for the church family and all who will believe because of our message (John 17:6- 26). It is the compassionate prayer of the Good Samaritan who responds to the hurting, dying and downtrodden.

The seeking prayer is a serious and urgent seeking of Kingdom living and the Father's will and direction for each day of service and witness. It surely must be answered because the model for this is our Lord himself. This is the vineyard prayer, "where do I work today Father?" It is a harvesters prayer, "Lord, the fields are white unto harvest; may I go to help with the reaping?" It is the partnership prayer of the church, "Lord, let me help our partners in the other boat". For there is a harvest where the Lord directs our efforts and only He can see the whole picture. The fishermen had fished all night in waters so familiar to them, but caught nothing! They may have been experts in fishing but only the Lord can save the lost. It was the lost and sick to whom he came. If we are prepared to really ask him he will show us Kingdom things and meet our needs at the same time. The fishermen were obedient, they got their catch and more than they could have ever hoped for. Their needs were met but so were countless families around the lakeside.

The loud persistent prayer (knocking) is the power prayer. We are not and cannot be Christians without the Lord, the Holy Spirit within us. We have no authority without his anointing upon us, we have no power without being cloaked in power from on high (Acts1:8). This is a prayer for action. No lukewarmness here. A car will not run without fuel. A gun cannot fire without a cartridge of explosives to launch the bullet. A fire will not light without a match and a bulb will not glow without electricity. This prayer releases in us the energy, power, authority and light of Christ to save a dark, powerless, rebellious and tired world. It is the Elijah prayer that turns dry ground into rain soaked land. It is revival praying.

In the two parts of this book, we shall explore practical examples of such prayers with examples from scripture.

ACKNOWLEDGEMENTS

My grateful thanks to my wife Joan and my daughters Julianne and Felicity for encouraging me to complete the writing of this book and for reading the chapters as they were finished and making many constructive suggestions to improve the reading. I also want to bless Julianne for her artwork that has captured the sense of the book wonderfully, and all of them for praying with me about it.

I must also record my thanks to William Porter, my friend and colleague, over many years as we have tried to share the revival vision God gave us for the UK Methodist Church at Blackpool Easter people in 1999, and who encouraged me to share something of the urgency I have for intercession by writing this book. I thank him too for his dedication to the task of editing it.

Members of my churches have helped so willingly with the typing, reading over and testimonies. Special thanks to Dorothy, Robin, Grace and a second Dorothy. They know who they are and of my great appreciation.

Lastly my thanks to Scott, Craig, Kevin and Paul who have found time in amongst busy schedules to read the book and write some words about it. They are great friends and men of God, who it is a pleasure and blessing to know.

Most of all I acknowledge the leading of the Spirit as He has guided my thoughts and remembrances and continued to give me insight and inspiration during the writing.

I have not stopped giving thanks for you, remembering you in my prayers. [Eph 1:16]

PART ONE

GOLDEN BOWLS OF INCENSE

Chapter 1
A New Song — The Church
(Revelation 5:1-14)

For our struggle is not against flesh and blood, but against the rulers, against the authorities, against the powers of this dark and against the spiritual forces of evil in the heavenly realms. (Ephesians 6:11)

"Thine be the glory, risen conquering Son, endless is the victory thou O'er death hast won." Edmond L Budry (1854-1932)

He put a new song in my mouth, a hymn of praise to our God. Many will see and fear and put their trust in the Lord. (Psalm 40:3)

In August 1996 I was in a United Methodist Church in Pine Forest, Florida for a Prayer Conference called by my friend Pastor Perry Dalton. I had never experienced anything like it before, even though my churches in the UK were entering a powerful time of renewal in the Spirit. It wasn't a slick, well advertised conference with glossy literature, but one where nearly two hundred pastors from the UMC gathered together with some 'interlopers' from the UK to seek God for revival in the United Methodist Church. It wasn't a big city church but a typical small United Methodist Church nestling in the suburbs of and caught up in the amazing move of God in Brownsville, Pensacola.

To call it a prayer conference was inaccurate, although I know that Perry distinctly heard from the Lord that he had to call it such. What happened was just amazing. My journal is full of notes, names, visions and answered prayer. I didn't, and couldn't return to the UK the same. I had been somewhere and seen something that almost defied description. That experience has been repeated on so many occasions in the UK, Europe, Singapore and USA in different buildings and fellowships since.

I recall also one concert of intercessory prayer at Brownsville when heaven seemed to open and our voices cried out to the Lord from all over the sanctuary. I was up in the balcony on my knees before a banner when a tongue that I didn't recognize broke free from my lips and I was lost in 'wonder, love and praise'. I found myself under the pews out on the floor when the prayers ended about an hour later! It has been my privilege to have that type of experience and on many other occasions too. mixture of wonder, praise, love, awe and celebration focused on and found only in Jesus. I think that it is a bit like what we read in this chapter from John's vision at Patmos. I am so inspired by it. It is a picture of The Church in love with and in awe of the Lamb, who has the victory.

In his book "'The Toronto Blessing' – An experience of Renewal and Revival", Guy Chevreau describes the nightly experience of people from all over the world with these words: *" Since the first of the meetings with Randy Clark on 20th January, 1994, the Airport Vineyard has been host to a renewing move of God that has brought a long awaited release of freedom and healing, joy and power. Protracted meetings have been* *held every night but Mondays. ………In the wake of a defeated, discouraged and characteristically exhausted Christian experience, thousands of believers have returned to their 'first love' (Rev 2:4). Many have experienced, with this restored intimacy with the Lord, a renewing commitment and call, an enlarging of spiritual vision, a rekindled passion for Jesus and the work of the Kingdom…."*

Since that time Guy Chevreau has gone on to write a number of inspiring books reflecting on and teaching about the experience of being in the presence of Jesus and seeing His glory being revealed around the world.

Pete Greig writes a very challenging and honest account of prayer and suffering in his book "God on Mute". Amongst many stories about real people and situations he shares a very personal testimony about discovering the power of prayer, whilst his wife (an epileptic) has a seizure in the car. He describes how at the first signs of the seizure he swung his van into a church car park, encouraged the two children to play in a convenient play area, and then began to attend to his wife. Whilst he was trying to help her with a breathing exercise, she managed to gasp, "pray!" through clenched teeth. Even though he admits that prayer had not made any difference before, he began to ask God to intervene. As he prayed his eyes fell on a poster outside the church. The poster showed Christ wearing a crown of thorns, and underneath was written something about 'the blood of the Lamb'. This is how his narrative continues *"More out of desperation than inspiration, I took the prompt and focused my attention on the power of Jesus' blood. That's when the most remarkable thing happened: The frenzy in Samie's arm halted its advance. Then, as I continued to pray, I watched as the spasms began to retreat back down her arm toward her hand. I could hardly believe what I was seeing. With mounting faith, I continued to pray, and soon the convulsions reached her hand and seemed to subside altogether.* "When his prayers lapsed the seizure began again and more prayer followed, this time with vigour and rising faith. In the end there was peace. Samie felt that she had encountered Jesus in her pain and a spiritual battle was won.

I mention these two examples because they illustrate why I think that this "New Song" of the Church is so vital to our prayer and intercession. The scene so described in Revelation 5 is such a powerful one, and as such, I think that God intends it to be the focus and end of our petitions. Four things are going on that are worthy of consideration.

Firstly it is set in the context of worship of the Godhead, which is described in Chapter 4.

Secondly it is focused on Jesus, the one who is worthy to receive all honour and glory. It is very Christo-centric because Jesus is described by his various titles: Lion of the tribe of Judah, the Root of David, the crucified Lamb, the victor in the battle against evil and the devil and, by taking the scroll, The Lord of Lords and King of kings.

Thirdly, all the prayers of the Saints are offered in worship to Jesus, in golden bowls, by the living creatures and the twenty four elders. Prayers of intercession offered to the great Intercessor.

Fourthly, a new song spontaneously erupts from the mouths of all those present, growing in power as innumerable voices are added until every creature in heaven and on earth and on the sea and all that is in them has joined in. It is a breathtaking revelation of the glory of the Lamb. New songs being sung, constant movement as the twenty four elders and four living creatures fall down before Jesus, and the angels encircle the throne while all creation sings his praise. Isn't that the reason why we would pray and intercede for our neighbourhood, our nations and the world? Doesn't this revelation capture our spirit and cause a cry of praise to escape our lips? Doesn't this encapsulate the promise of salvation for all people? I'd say that it does.

Perhaps it does more than that too. I think that it reveals the heart of prayer that touches the heart of God. The new song is in itself a prayer, or series of prayers. I love many of the songs from the IHOP (international House of Prayer) and the World Prayer Centre. They are sung prayer and I am sure touch the heart of God. I bless those who persevere in prayer 24/7 for us in all the Houses of Prayer. In his forward to 'The Sound of Heaven' worship CD, Terry MacAlmon writes these words, " The sound of heaven – what an amazing and beautiful sound that cannot be counterfeited by the enemy. It's the sound like that of many rushing waters and peals of thunder; It's the sound of the redeemed giving back worship to their

Saviour. It's a sound like none other, anywhere." Amen and amen! I think too that Terry captures something of the New Song in his very anointed song called "Holy are You Lord" (copyright 1997 TMMI Music). The words are as follows:-

> Hear the sound of heaven
> Like the sound of many waters
> It's the sound of worship
> Coming from the throne.
> Cries of adoration
> As men of every nation
> Lift their voice to make His glory known, singing
> Holy, holy, holy are You Lord
> Holy, holy, holy are You Lord
> The angels and the elders bow
> The redeemed worship You now
> Holy, holy, holy are You Lord

The prayers of the heavenly beings, the Saints and all creatures reveal to us a number of subjects for prayer, namely:-

> The worthiness of Jesus (v9a)
>
> The victory of the cross (v9b)
>
> The inclusiveness of his death and resurrection (v9c)
>
> The plan and purpose of God for all the redeemed (v9d)
>
> The glorious nature of God (v12)
>
> The eternal reign of God (v13b)

To which the response is Amen – nothing more to be said! (v14)

In these opening visions of the Book of Revelation we are shown that the victory of Christ has already been won. That victory was won on earth. The heaven of this vision is, most likely, to be the 'heavenly places' of Paul's letter to the Ephesians (1:3,20) because the vision includes the present creation and a church still living on earth and needing to have communion with God through prayer (Rev 5:8,10, &13). It is these prayers that help bring about fulfilment of the new creation, new heaven and new earth and Jesus' eternal kingdom.

I love the description of the heavenly realm given by G. B. Caird in *"The Revelation of St John the Divine"* (A. and C. Black 1966) when he writes: "By the voice of 4:1 John 'is summoned to the control room at Supreme Headquarters…a room lined with maps, in which someone has placed clusters of little flags…It is war time, and the flags represent units of a military command. The movement of flags may mean one of two things: either because changes have taken place on the battlefield, with which the maps must be made to agree, or that an order is being issued for troop movements, and the flags are being moved to the new positions the units are expected to occupy……"

This interpretation of the heavenly realm being like Supreme Headquarters resonates with the understanding that the spiritual warfare we are engaged is for the salvation of the lost. It is good, too, as it will be replaced for certain by the permanent headquarters of God, heaven itself, in a lasting peace.

This is why I have chosen this title "Golden Bowls of Incense" because it overarches all the types of prayer that I want to share with you. Furthermore, it is what empowers and inspires me to intercessory prayer. May it be so for you too.

Time is short. The western world is in moral and ethical darkness. Christian belief and practice is under remorseless attack. God is mocked by the media, science, the establishment and an increasingly agnostic people. Now is the time to fill the golden bowls with our prayers. Let me finish by sharing a sobering vision of the future in a passage from "The Church Invisible" by Nick Page, subtitled 'A journey into the future of the UK church'.

'There are no village churches left now,' she said. 'There was one left up in Yorkshire, but it went a few months ago. It's a kitchen salesroom now, or a sushi bar. I forget which. All the rest have been knocked down, or turned into bars, clubs, sports halls, museums.' She gestured around her. 'Or houses.'

'But what happens when people want to get married?' I asked. 'And what about christenings or funerals?'

She smiled. 'No-one gets married any more,' she said, 'No-one makes promises these days.' She sighed. 'I often think that that was one of the main things the church had to teach people: what it meant to keep promises.'

'What about burials?'

'The Government banned then several years ago, because of the shortage of land. Now everyone is biodynamically recycled.'

'Er ...I'm sorry?'

She shook her head. 'You don't want to know the details.'

'It sounds a bit like cremation ...'I guessed.

'No, she replied, 'I should say it's more like composting.'

'Oh.' I thought for a moment. She was right. I didn't want to know the details. I tried to concentrate on the other end of the spectrum. 'What about christenings?'

'Don't be daft! How can people be welcomed into a church that no longer exists? No, all the rituals have been lost.' She shook her head. 'You know when I was young I never understood that people needed ritual. I used to despise it rather. Now, there is no ritual anymore. I can see how it is sorely missed. Of course, some people still have their children christened. Mr Henderson down the other end has got the font in his living room, so people still pay him money to have their child dunked. They're trying to "rediscover" traditional England. For then it's like taking up Morris Dancing or smoking a clay pipe.'

'For many people in our day it was more or less the same,' I said.

'Perhaps. But at least there was always the hope that something would come out of that contact.'

'So what happened?' I asked, 'Where did it all go wrong? How could the church just disappear this way?'

She sighed.

'There are many reasons,' she said. 'As you will no doubt find. But if you ask me, I think the primary reason was that we forgot how to be different.'

'What do you mean?'

'The church is here – was here, I should say – to show people what God is like. Didn't you used to say that yourself?'

Let us come before Him in humble and fervent praise. To pray for our communities and nation so that the flags on the map at Supreme HQ are moved to reflect heaven touching and transforming earth through the blood of the Lamb. To God be the glory.

Chapter 2

Perseverance pays off — **Elijah** (James 5: 17-18)

Elijah was a man, just like us. He prayed earnestly that it would not rain, and it did not rain on the land for three and a half years. Again he prayed, and the heavens gave rain, and the earth produced its crops (James 5:17-18)

"When you put the iron down with the right principles, and the heat comes from the iron, the wrinkles come out. It's a good example of effective fervent prayer. So what is fervency? It is turning the iron on. It's getting some heat into your prayers. (Effective Fervent Prayer – Mary Alice Isleib)

"And \[pray] also for me, that [freedom of] utterance may be given me, that I may open my mouth to declare it boldly and courageously, as I ought to do. (Ephesians 6:18 Amplified Bible)

Perseverance: steadfast pursuit of and aim, constant persistence O.E.D.

When the Anglican (C of E) church in Britain told Rev Canon Andrew White that his multiple sclerosis made him too ill to minister, he became the 'Vicar of Baghdad'. Even though many in his congregation have been murdered, including a family he baptized in January 2009, Andrew continues to love his mission in Iraq. He says " before the war our church was not allowed to function. Tariq Aziz, the then deputy Prime Minister, did let me take services there when I was present. I now have the largest church in Iraq. It is all Iraqi and not one person is traditionally Anglican. We even have our own clinic with three doctors and three dentists and a brilliant pharmacist and pharmacy thank to the British Charity International Health Partners. Most of the patients are not even Christians but people come to church to be healed. Now Jesus would have liked that! ......when I started running this church it cost $600 a year. Now it costs $83,000 a month. We have to totally support our people with food, rent, money and health care.....our people have nothing, but with the help of our Lord and his people, we manage. We never know where the money will come from but with God's help it comes in."

I was so moved when I heard Andrew say this during a sermon at one of my churches that tears silently ran down my face. He said it, not in any boasting way, but with a deep integrity of faith and love. I marvelled at this contemporary example of God answering effective fervent prayer.

In my last circuit a group of intercessors prayed for over 5 years, meeting almost every week to intercede for renewal in a village church that had almost ceased to exist. We persevered in praise and prayer until there was a breakthrough in the spiritual atmosphere of the building. When we felt the sweet presence of the Lord we began to receive 'pictures'; and 'words' from God and direction for the church. From that time we have moved to a position today of employing a lay evangelist to lead our mission to the village and, we have, against all odds, found funds for a new extension to the building so that our facilities are up to date and glorify God. With only 8 members (3 working) that is a miracle brought about by persistence!

In one of my previous churches, the men's prayer group used to meet on a Saturday morning, quite early. We would usually gather for toast and a cup of tea at 7.00am then begin to pray from 7.30 – 9.00am. Our assignment was to pray for men. We had two lists of names of men, mostly the husbands of women in the church, or men whom we knew and felt God tell us to pray for. We had a 'first eleven' and a reserve eleven. As a man became a Christian we would take him off the list and add one from the reserve list. We persevered with this for about five years and in that time saw at least eleven men come to faith. We really held them up before God. Some men were very indifferent to the Church and Christianity and we wept before God for them to be softened and we wept again with joy when they came to love Jesus.

There are two different examples of fervent, persevering prayer. One is of the Lord himself (*In the days of His flesh [Jesus] offered up definite, special petitions [for that which He not only wanted but needed] and supplications with strong crying and tears to Him. Who was [always] able to save Him [out] from death, and He was heard because of His reverence towards God [His godly fear, His piety, in that He shrank from the horrors of separation from the bright presence of the Father.]* (Hebrews 5:7 Amplified Bible). The other is that of Elijah.

Elijah's prayers for drought can be found in 1 Kings 17:1 and then for rain in 1 Kings 18:1, 41-46. But Elijah wasn't praying for the sake of a miracle of nature or for his own glory. The evil of Ahab, the king of Israel, moved him to seek God for Ahab's downfall and that of his wicked wife Jezebel. He began by reminding Ahab of God 's sovereignty and His, Elijah's, anointing as a Prophet of God. He demonstrated that he had the ear of God by having the authority to declare a drought. A drought would be catastrophic for Israel and also expose Jezebel and Ahab's wickedness. Elijah was looking for regime change, It came about but not the way that the West has used it in the latter half of the twentieth century.

James, the Lord's brother, in his letter to the churches, refers to Elijah's prayer life and in particular, his persevering fervent prayer. He confirms what all believing Jews would have learnt, that is, that Elijah prayed in a drought and then prayed in the rain. It is an amazing revelation that easily passes us by when thinking about the preceding verses, but is there to reinforce the need for effective fervent prayer, whether for healing or for regime change. It is a spiritual necessity to release the power and purpose of God into situations. It is not a quick prayer, or a 24/7 prayer for a week but fervent and persevering prayer that might take years as opposed to minutes, to move the hand of God.

In the example of Jesus' prayer (Hebrews 5:7) the Greek κραυγε (krauge: *shout, outcry, clamour, angry shouting)* suggests not just strong crying, but times when Jesus shrieked out, possibly screamed or most certainly cried loudly in prayer. I suppose also that there is an anguish of soul at times, which Jesus certainly experienced. A young man wonderfully converted during a Rob Frost mission to the York and Hull District of the Methodist Church in England used to enjoy sharing his new found scriptural knowledge, by asking what the shortest verse in the bible was. The answer he would proudly announce was "Jesus wept" (John 11:35). Although the Greek word 'to weep' is not the same as in Hebrews 5:7, I personally think that here too was a fervent prayer for Lazarus to be raised and for the last enemy, death, to be defeated for his friend.

In the case of Elijah, the Greek adverb which translates "to pray earnestly" means that Elijah's soul went gushed out in prayer. I suppose it really means that he gave all of himself in prayer. He was fervent. He was on fire for God in the power of the Spirit and he heard from God and delivered God's word. His prayer changed a nation by exposing an evil regime, and foretelling its principal's demise. That is what God intends fervent prayer will do.

God plants in our hearts a deep yearning and a passion for His kingdom and His holiness. He lets us experience the pain of seeing evil and corrupt authorities persecute God's people and obstruct His purposes. When this happens our prayers become fervent, intense and powerful in the Holy Spirit. It is clear that God who dwells in us by His Spirit is jealous for us and his plans for us. As such this releases a fervency within us. In James 4:5 we are told *"or do you think Scripture says without reason that the Spirit He caused to live in us envies intensely?"* (NIV) or, as the Amplified Bible puts it, *"He yearns for the Spirit to be welcomed with a jealous love?"*

So Elijah believed and persevered. Seven times he sent his servant to look for rain clouds when there had been none. Sometimes we know what God's plan is because He has promised us in His word or He has given us a prophetic revelation or vision. Elijah knew rain would come – he said to Ahab, *"Go, eat and drink, for there is the sound of a heavy rain"* (1 Ki 19:41). Elijah didn't see it or smell the rain at that moment but he took hold of God's promise by faith and prayed it into being.

God has promised salvation for all who will believe. He has promised to pour out His Spirit on all flesh. He has promised seasons of refreshing. He wants all people to be saved.

Let us get on our knees to change the political, economic, social and moral conditions in our nation and persevere until the rain clouds come.

Dave Wellington captures the prayer in his song, written in 1995 "Send us the rain, Lord" (Copyright KIngsways, Thank You music)

> SEND US THE RAIN, LORD,
>
> Rain of Your spirit,
> Rain on this dry barren land.
> Send us the rain, Lord
> Rain to revive us;
> Cleanse us and fill us again.
> Here we are, of one accord,
> Calling to You, singing:
> Send Your Spirit,
> Send Your Spirit,
> Send the rain on us again.

Amen, send the rain Lord.

Chapter 3

HEZEKIAH –
Strong men lay hold of the kingdom

"Augustine once said that God puts salt on the tongue so that we may thirst for Him. Sometimes perhaps it is our own tears that carry the salt. (Pete Greig/Dave Roberts in Red Moon Rising)

"Prosperity dost best discover vice and adversity doth best discover virtue." Francis Bacon

---

In his insightful book on spiritual warfare called "The Three Battlegrounds," Francis Frangipane *writes: "It will take a city wide church to win the city wide war. Our separate, isolated efforts will not stop the flood of increasing evil in our cities if we, as Christ's church, remain isolated from each other. "*

How true! When nations are prosperous and over-confident in worldly policies and politics they ignore spiritual values with the result that innumerable sins against God and humanity flow. This is the moment before collapse, the moment that a determined enemy attacks the kingdom of God. Divine judgement is the result of self-centredness and rebellion.

When the church is not led by and united in the Spirit, there is a weakness in our warfare and it will take strong men and women (spiritually speaking) to hold up the arms of the church in prayer for victory over evil (see Ex 17:8-13).

Among movers and shakers today are the intercessors, the prayer warriors and those with the prophetic voice into governments. We are blessed on both sides of the Atlantic with such people and groups.

I thank God for Interprayer and Brian Mills, for Jane Holloway (WPC) and global day of prayer, MET and Ignite Revival Network. The 2C7 group in Stoke-on-Trent in the UK and Methodist intercessions in USA, Singapore and Europe. Also John and Carol Arnott for their "soaking" network (CFM) and also International Houses of Prayer, Trumpet Call, and many intercessions groups.

Hezekiah was such a man for his time (that is 7th Century BC).

What do we know about him? (from 2 Kings 18-20 & Isaiah 36)

- Co-Regent at 25 (line of David) with his mother.
- Sole King at 54 yrs in 715BC.
- 14 year reign until 686BC.
- Followed Ahaz, whose rule according to the prophesy in Isaiah 3:1-16 caused the country to be the rudderless ship of State.
- When Sennacherib (King of Assyria) captured the 46 fortified cities of Judah and took over 200,000 prisoners, Hezekiah became a prisoner in his own palace — like a "bird in a cage" (2 Kings 18:12).

What sort of man was he? Firstly he did what was right in the eyes of the Lord (2 Kings 18:4) God's anger was stirred up against Judah because of its' sins under Jeroboam (1 Kings 14: 6-11). Specifically Hezekiah: a) removed the high places dedicated to the worship of idols, b) smashed sacred stones. c) cut down the asherah poles, and d) broke the bronze snake (Nehustan) because people worshipped it, particularly during the reign of the apostate Ahab.

Secondly, he trusted in the Lord, the God of Israel (2 Kings 18:5). He held fast to the Lord and did not hesitate to follow Him (2 Kings 18:6). Thirdly, he kept the commandments that the Lord had given to Moses. He worshipped in Solomon's temple that he restored as pre-eminent. As a result he was successful in all that he undertook and he was also the target of the enemy.

> There was no-one like him among all the Kings of Judah, either before him or after him (2 Kings 18:5)

Despite that accolade in scripture it does not mean that ordinary people like us are excused from such an assignment in our generation. Listen to the prayer of Count Zinzendorf (founder of the Moravian movement in the 18th century) *"May there still be thousands of them, who in the planned and way assigned them, and in the orders in to which you have called them, without leaving their way of worship and founding a new church for themselves, prove their identity as inward men of God, as members of your invisible and true body before all people for Your own sake. Amen"* (quoted in Red Moon Rising p62)

In October 2004 in the European Parliament there was a remorseless attack on the character and ability of Rocco Buttiglione, the justice and internal affairs minister, who said that homosexuality is a sin and doubted the ability of single mothers to bring up fully adjusted children. Buttiglione, an Italian Catholic Christian, was in his own way daring to be like Hezekiah within the European Parliament. The verbal abuse and political manoeuvrings of the liberal and socialist MEP's to vote down the Italian Presidency of the EU and secure Mr Buttiglione's removal has been a modern example of the spiritual battles facing Hezekiah.

In many ways we see this repeated again and again in both the UK and the USA where the Christian faith and church is under a continuous attack by and through controversial legislation that highlights religious differences between the moral and ethical standards of, on the one hand Bible believing conservative Christians and a liberal non-believing religious pluralism on the other.

Within the Church too we are seeing a growing divide between evangelicals and liberals. The ordination of practising homosexual clergy is, for many, the final straw. Idolatry, false worship, rebellion, religious pluralism and increasing secularisation of the church are part of a war of attrition on Christianity waged through the Media, Europe, the Government and parts of the church, in which, like Hezekiah, those Christians who seek to be faithful to scripture and the commands of Jesus, find themselves to be prisoners in their 'Jerusalem', like birds in a cage.

Moreover the suffering Church in other parts of the world grows under the twin tyrants of religious hatred and persecution, with violence, murder, rape and hostage taking, increasingly fuelled by those hostile to both truth and love. The attack is allowed to be more violent because the western church is in no position to speak with one evangelical voice or to act in the power of the Holy Spirit. It is apparently not now acceptable to speak out the gospel of Christ nor to apply the moral and ethical values of the kingdom of God in Government, society, work or schools.

If we think that this is a modem phenomenon only, then let us look at what happened to Hezekiah. He faced two challenges, firstly from Sennacherib's commander and secondly from Sennacherib himself.

Assyria was used by God to punish Israel (Isaiah 10:5-6) and now Sennacherib (The Great King — Isaiah 36:4) challenges Jerusalem and Judah to submit to him, His plan is twofold. Firstly to persuade the people to ignore the godly Hezekiah (despite knowing all the good things that Hezekiah has done for his people and for God) and secondly to ridicule the God of the Jews (Isaiah 36:4-22).

Sennacherib personally enters the fray (Isa 37:9-13). In his declarations he both mocks God and then brags about Assyrian power and victories as proof that he does not need God.

Hezekiah's response to imprisonment, invasion, and threat is informative and instructive for us. This is what he does:

He repents on behalf of the nation and puts on sackcloth and seeks the Lord in prayer and worship (Isa 37:1) Then he involves his officials (Isa 37:2) and finally sends for the prophet of God so he can hear from God and take appropriate action(Isa 37:2).

He hears from God and begins his petition by firstly laying it before the Lord in the temple (Isa 37:14) and offers prayers of adoration and praise *(Is 37: 15-16)*. Then he moves to the specific problem at hand, the insult and action of the Assyrians, and asks God to help (cf Acts 4) whilst in faith declaring the Lord's supremacy. He sets the proper context for his trust in the Lord (vv 8-19) and asks for deliverance (v20a) and the glory of God (v20b)

The good news is that God answered! Hallelujah!

God answers through Isaiah the prophet who initiates the word of the Lord by sending a messenger to Hezekiah (Isaiah 37:21). God has replied because Hezekiah prayed! Hezekiah received three words from the Lord:

- Against Sennacherib (Isaiah 37:22-29): God condemns him for daring to insult and blaspheme him. God makes it clear that he (God) is in charge from the beginning - God punishes Sennacherib.

- For Hezekiah (Isaiah 37:30-32): a three year plan for restoration, in which a new nation will arise through God's promise.

- For Jerusalem (Isaiah 37:33-35): the zeal of the Lord accomplishes their freedom and gives a new start (Isaiah 37:36-38)

As a modern example of God removing obstacles and releasing His favour take the Beacon House of Prayer, in Stoke on Trent. When William Porter and a small group of committed Christians established their prayer base in Tunstall, Stoke-on-Trent in 2006, their search for suitable premises led them to a small, modernised building with a showroom on the ground floor and a basement space underneath. As they began to pray for the city and worship God they discovered that they shared the building with a brothel whose employees used the first floor room above the worship area and had a separate entrance next door. With no room to expand or space to have counselling and healing rooms, an office or kitchen, they continued to worship God and pray for the city, its lost and broken, its children and young people. At the end of 2008 the landlord offered them the former brothel lease and a large industrial garage at the rear. They now have even better facilities for 24/7 prayer and ministry. God also opened the door to local children in the Junior school to visit the building to pray and touch the presence of God. The worship leader and his team are also now regularly leading praise at the local secondary school, leading teenagers into the arms of a loving God and Father.

Strong men lay hold of the Kingdom. Let us not be discouraged, but, like Hezekiah, shift our gaze from the problem, onto the God for whom nothing is impossible. To God be the glory, great things He has done and will do.

Chapter 4
"Called to Action"
Nehemiah [Nehemiah **1: 3-11]**

"He closed down five hundred English houses of prostitution. He raised such a protest over the scheduled heavyweight boxing match between American Jack Johnson and Bombardier Wells that the event was cancelled. He went in to the window washing business and the lumber business to provide work for unemployed labourers. He formed a prison aid society that fed breakfast to thousands of just-released prisoners who had no place to go but the nearest tavern. He established a savings bank for ex-convicts and erected a Provident House to provide them with living quarters. He actively supported the temperance movement, and travelled on missionary journeys to South Africa and inland." FB**.** Meyer was called to action by God at the age of l6.
Spiritual Power — Sherwood Elliot Wirt: *Lion Books*

"For more than fifty years Wesley recorded in his journal the work he undertook. It is the diary of an activist par excellence. The narrative throbs with energy and leaves the reader struggling to keep up with the comings and goings, the doings and writings, the preaching, teaching, praying, organising and reorganising of the human dynamo at the centre of revival. It is a day by day account of God at work in conversion.
Evangelical Spirituality — James M. Gordon: *SPCK*

Whenever there is a great work of God, someone has been called to action and has got on with it.

The story of Nehemiah *is* one of those accounts from which "Boys Own" stories are made of. An apparently insignificant man moved to great exploits against all the odds. The difference between this and the comic book story is a six-letter word PRAYER.

This story is important for us today because it is a revival story, a miracle story and an amazing story all rolled into one. Its origins and power are found in the prayers of a devout and humble man, exiled from his own country, called Nehemiah.

Nehemiah's prayers and action teach us today that when we care enough about the spiritual life of our nation and cry over the unfaithfulness of the Church and desire only for God to be glorified, then God will put us to work with Him, to bring revival. Just as Nehemiah would have been struck by the accuracy of Isaiah's prophecy of the destruction and exile of Judah and Jerusalem (Isaiah 1 — 5), so we need to heed the prophetic word about our church and nation today. Consider, for example, the prophetic voice crying out for the children of our country.

Today we are witnessing the tragedy of systematic and remorseless damage being inflicted upon the lives of children and young people world-wide. Our personal and collective responsibility for what is now happening to our children in this country and throughout the world cannot be denied. Despite all our many concerns and endeavours the cruel fact remains that by any standard of judgment we are failing them.

This statement spells out the chilling evidence of what we are doing to our children today.

The truth is that we are robbing them of their dignity and innocence. We are exploiting them. We are forcing adult ideas upon them. We are abusing and confusing them. We are depriving them of faith and a moral framework for life. We are deliberately putting our interests and rights as adults before theirs as children. We are failing to recognise their vulnerability and the truth that vast numbers of them live in fear and loneliness and are deeply damaged. We are depriving them of love and security. We are polluting their minds and teaching them vulgarity in language and lifestyle. We are desensitizing them to violence. We are poisoning them with squalid and degrading sexual images. We are implanting into our children wrong standards - greed, lust, violence, dirtiness. bad manners, lack of consideration for others and lack of respect for themselves.

Whilst our children are being corrupted by the standards of a selfish, materialistic society, most of us remain deafeningly silent.

"What on earth are we doing to our children?

Maranatha Community 1995

446 years before the birth of Christ, in the city of Susa (the major city of Elam — modern-day south-west Iran) Nehemiah, together with many of his countrymen, is in exile. Following Nebuchadnezzar's destruction of Jerusalem and the capture of its people in 597 BC, the people of Judah have been exiled in parts of Babylon. The prophets Jeremiah, Habakkuk and Obadiah prophesied during this time. The book of Lamentations is virtually our only source of information about conditions in Jerusalem during the exile. The conditions were appalling. But however desperate the condition of life was in Jerusalem for the people who lived there, this was not as great as the disgrace experienced by the people because of their unfaithfulness to God in worship and righteous living. The sorrow of the people in captivity is summed up in Psalms like Psalm 137

"By the rivers of Babylon we sat down and wept when we remembered Zion. " (v1) "How can we sing the songs of the Lord while in a foreign land? If I forget you, 0 Jerusalem, may my right hand forget its skill. May my tongue cling to the roof of my mouth if do not remember you. If I do not consider Jerusalem my highest joy." (vv4-6)

Nehemiah would have shared these feelings, despite being born in exile, for his birthright was God's inheritance, the promised land, and Jerusalem, once queen among the provinces (Lamentations 1:2). The impossibility of restoring Jerusalem and its people from such disaster would seem to be an distant dream. But God had a plan. It was an amazing plan to use a foreign emperor to be his anointed one to end the exile (Is 45: 1) and to be a shepherd of Israel to accomplish what God was pleased to do - namely to rebuild the temple and Jerusalem (Is.44:28). Therefore following the capture of Babylon by Cyrus, the Persian, many of his countrymen had returned to Judah and Jerusalem. Ezra, the priest had led a second party back in 458 BC following the rebuilding of the temple in 516 BC and had restored the worship in the temple. The city and its walls, however, were still in ruins. Cyrus had been replaced by Xerxes, who in turn was succeeded by Artaxerxes. Work on the city had been stopped due to opposition from the Persian governors in a letter to Artaxerxes (Ezra 4: 12) and Artaxerxes' order (Ezra 4:21). The city and its people were defenceless against attacks by their enemies. (Theucydides described the comparable condition of Athens after its devastation by the Persians in 480-479BC). In 446 BC Nehemiah hears word from his brother Hanani, "Those who survived the exile are back in the province and are in great trouble and disgrace. The wall of Jerusalem is broken down, and its gates have been burned with fire." (Neh. 1:3) This is the point in time when God hears Nehemiah's cry for the plight of God's people and converts it, through prayer, into the action needed to fulfil the penultimate part of Jerusalem's restoration. God's revival pattern is to restore in sequence — Temple; Purity; Safety; Word.

The result is that the walls are rebuilt, the gates restored and set in place. The integrity of Jerusalem and the unity and safety of her people is assured, and they are ready to receive the word.

Nehemiah's prayer is an example of the task-orientated prayer, a fivefold approach to God, in order to save the Church, restore her integrity and build up her strength and calling as a "sign and a wonder of God's presence in the world" (Isaiah 8: 18)

Nehemiah's prayer pattern in chapter one is:

I. "What can I do?" prayer — verse 3
II. "What do I say?" Arrow prayers — verse 4
III. "What do I do?" prayers — verse 12
IV. "Give us victory" prayers — Ch 4 verses 4-5
V. "Protect us" prayers — Ch 4 verse 9

Nehemiah needed his prayer relationship with God. The work to which he was being called was literally front line work. What could be more front line than to rebuild the walls of Jerusalem and to set the twelve gates in place? What could be more calculated to cause confrontation with Israel and Judah's enemies than to re-establish the security of the Holy City and the protection of its inhabitants? What could threaten the neighbouring states more than the people of God becoming, once again, a faithful, worshipping and united people? What challenges Satan more than the glory of God being revealed in and through his people with signs and wonders? Nehemiah was God's man for this moment, and he knew that God would accomplish what he had promised to do (see Neh. 6:16).

Hudson Taylor, the great missionary of the China Inland Mission said that on the threshold of his great lifework,

God said to him, *"My child, I'm going to evangelise inland China, and if you would like to walk with Me I will do it through you."*

We too are called to be like Nehemiah. So let us begin to join with God's will and His miracle working power for our nation through a fivefold approach to God in prayer.

> ### The "What can I do?" prayers
> (Proverbs 11:23; Rmns 10: 1)

Now is the time to reach the heart and ear of God through genuine prayers of intercession to end the disgrace of the Church. Jesus said 'Blessed are those who acknowledge their spiritual poverty for they share in the salvation of the Kingdom of God and they will be comforted as they pray for those who are dead to sin!' Matt,5: 3- 4), The prayer of a righteous man is powerful and effective (James 5:16) This is both a prayer of repentance and a prayer for forgiveness (Neh. 1:4-11) It is a fervent prayer (1 Thess 5:17). it is a persevering prayer, it is a bold prayer (Luke 11:5-8). Notice that Nehemiah does not simply pray for the rest of his people. He repents on behalf of himself and his family, because he sees himself as being involved in the sins of Israel. Even though he was born during the exile he shares the common identity of the exiles. What they have done in the past, he has done, what they are, he is. So it is with us too. When the three thousand responded to Peter's Pentecost sermon they said "What shall we do?" Peter urged them to repent and be baptised, in the name of Jesus, for the forgiveness of their sins. Even though they were sinful people who had not kept a true love for God, they knew, like Nehemiah, that God keeps covenant and steadfast love with his people and therefore they could call upon him.

The " What do I say?" prayer
(cf. Matt. 10:19-20)

There are many times that we don't know how to begin to speak about what is on our heart to other people. We don't want to compromise our faith or upset someone or to be misunderstood. In these cases we look to the Lord — not in long pious prayer but short pleadings for help - arrow prayers. It would be wrong to suppose that these are just asking for words for the sake of something to say. They are not. These prayers are asking for the *rhema* word upon which so much depends, as with the shepherds' hearing of Jesus birth from the angels (Luke 2:15). In practical terms it is asking God by his Spirit to totally guide what we are to say so that it will accomplish his will and purpose. These are the prayers for when we speak to a total stranger, or someone that we would find it hard to share our faith with, or even an enemy.

The "What do I do?'" prayers

Having asked God what can I do and say, Nehemiah reveals in this little aside "I set out during the night with a few men. I had not told anyone what my God had put in my heart to do for Jerusalem." (2:12) Certainly Nehemiah was being very cautious and discreet, not making known what he was up to (just as Jeremiah had been cautious with Zedekiah before the fall of Jerusalem - Jer. 38: 14ff cf. Mark 10:16). But the real point here is that God had spoken into Nehemiah's heart an understanding of exactly what needed to be done and how to do it. This could only have come about by constant prayer and communion with God. Nehemiah knows what to do. We need the Holy Spirit to tell us what to do. He is our guide He will only tell us what he hears from the heart of God and the mind of Christ. He will tell us what is to come and he will bring glory to Jesus.(John 16.13ff). Through the Holy Spirit, the disciples' grief turns to joy. The same happens to Nehemiah and the people of Jerusalem.

This prayer is vital. A corner stone on the rebuilt temple read, in Babylonian, *'I started building it weeping, but finished it rejoicing* ". However impossible the task seems, it becomes possible when God puts the plan on our heart and is completed when we act upon it. Nehemiah started off weeping but ended up rejoicing. What a prayer!

The "Give us victory "prayer

This is a prayer to be ready to pray as we are doing what God has laid on our heart. St. Paul reminded the Church that we will be engaged in spiritual warfare as we obediently serve God in the power of the Spirit

(Ephesians 6: 1-11). We will come under attack in many ways, from within as well as outside the church. The attack will be verbal, physical, emotional and spiritual. It will involve our families and friends. Every means will be used to stop us or divert us from the welfare of God's people. [Hb. Tobah].? Nehemiah experienced this. In the midst of all the taunts and threats, instead of turning to argue with the opposition, he turns to God in prayer. God answers the prayer and we read in chapter 4:6 that the work continued despite the opposition because the people worked with all their heart. This prayer does two things. Firstly it silences the opposition and secondly it builds up the resolve of God's people. That way, things get done much quicker! To God be the glory.

"Protect us" prayers

Lastly, but by no means least, comes the prayer that is needed to protect all the workers until the task is completed. This is the spiritual version of what is being provided through the very walls themselves. Nehemiah, inspired by the Spirit of God, has everyone praying together (4:9). This joins the people together in faith and obedience. It increases fellowship, it nurtures hope. This is the pastor's prayer with his people. The sheep with their shepherd, safe under his watch and care. This prayer is a powerful witness to the non-believers. The watch is maintained on the walls and on the people. They are kept safe. Rested and refreshed, day by day, they can joyfully share in the culmination of their efforts, the rebuilding of Jerusalem's walls and the glory of God present again amongst His people.

Revival leaders are often men and women like Nehemiah. They are humble, God-fearing people who bear a cup of prayer to the King of Kings and in so doing are mightily used by God to rebuild faith and fellowship. It was said that Nehemiah built faith and walls whilst Ezra built a 'church'.

'O Lord, God of heaven, the great and awesome God, who keeps his covenant of love with those who love him and obey his commands. Let your ear be attentive and your eyes open to hear the prayer your servant is praying before you day and night for your servants, the people of Israel." (Nehemiah 1:5-6a)

"Cities are central to God's redemptive strategy. The Great Commission begins with a city, Jerusalem – and culminates when another city, the new Jerusalem, becomes God's eternal dwelling with His people. In order to fulfil the Great Commission we must reach every city on earth with the gospel". As Ed Silvoso says in his book "That none should perish" (*Regal*):

Let us be empowered by God to move out in faith and prayer into what he calls us at this time.

Chapter 5

Can a nation be saved? - Abraham
(Genesis 18:16-33)

'As the solemn words, a revived church, the only hope for a dying world, are borne in upon us and burnt into us, prayer and intercession will become a transaction with God, in which our utter helplessness will have to take hold of and cling to His almighty power, and our whole life become possessed by the thought that there is nothing worth living for but the will of God in the salvation of man."
(Andrew Murray in *'The coming revival'*)

"The difference between prayer as we usually conceive it, and the kind that the early church practised is as vast as the difference between swimming in the bath tub as opposed to swimming in the open ocean."
(Ed Silvoso in *"That None Should Perish')*

'Let us then approach the throne of grace with confidence, so that we may receive mercy and find grace to help us in our time of need.' (Heb 4:16)

Sometimes God gets a hold of us during intercession and shows us things that break our hearts for our town or city or even our region or nation. He shares with us something of his heart for the salvation of the world. We may see visions of many falling into the pit of hell or hear God speaking about the evil in society that is a stench in His nostrils.

These are powerful times when we are called into the court of God and galvanised into fervent prayer. Other times we just know that things are far from right with society and the nation and so we pray as scripture commands us for the government and those in authority. We do this obediently and devotedly because we align ourselves to the conviction that God wants the world to be saved and has called us into this mission with him.

Either way, we begin to see the bigger picture. It is about the Kingdom of God, eternity, life and the glory of God. As a result of this we see the urgency of the hour to petition God for the salvation of our nation.

God, speaking through the prophet Ezekiel (22:30) says this *'I looked for a man among them who would build up the wall and stand before me in the gap on behalf of the land so I would not have to destroy it…'* So the answer to the question posed in this chapter might well be for God to say *'Yes, if you will humble yourselves before me, seek my face, confess your sins and turn from your wicked ways..'* (see 2 Chron.7:14f) So what do we learn from Abraham's pleading with God for Sodom and Gomorrah?

In the case of Abraham and God at Mamre, we have a wonderful example of how to pray for the nation. Abraham is in covenant relationship with God and he is visited by three men, from whom God speaks. I believe that God, Father Son and Holy Spirit are represented here by the three men. I think this is so because the urgency of the hour is so great for the salvation of

Sodom and Gomorrah. God is really serious about His people and their salvation. It is his divine purpose and only he can save them. The same is true today for us as children of the new covenant to whom God speaks and with whom He is present. God had previously spoken to Abraham about becoming "a father of many nations" and now visits Abraham to tell him of the miracle birth of a son in a year. This covenant promise is the seed of the birth of God's people, children of righteousness and of the promise bringing together in one family those who believe in Him, and who, themselves, are to be born again by the Spirit.

As God is about to leave Abraham, he tells Abraham of his mission to destroy Sodom and Gomorrah because of their grievous sin. He tells Abraham that the outcry in the heavenlies is so great against Sodom and Gomorrah that he has to see it for himself and then take action. (v17) God raises the subject himself and waits to see the response.

This immediately brings to my mind the song written by Gerald Coates (of Pioneer Churches fame) and Noel Richards (a gifted worship leader) written in 1992before either the Toronto outpouring, the Brownville Revival or the many revival moves of God around the world. The song is called "Great is the Darkness that covers the earth" I repeat it here by kind permission of Kingsway.

Golden Bowls of Incense

Great is the darkness that covers the earth.
Oppression, injustice and pain.
Nations are slipping in hopeless despair
Though many have come in your name.
Watching while sanity dies.
Touched by the madness and lies.

Come, Lord Jesus,
Come, Lord Jesus,
Pour out your Spirit we pray.
Come, Lord Jesus,
Come, Lord Jesus,
Pour out your Spirit on us today.

May now your church rise with power and love,
This glorious gospel proclaim.
In every nation salvation will come
To those who believe in your name.
Help us bring light to this world
That we might speed your return

Great celebrations on that final day
When out of the heavens you come.
Darkness will vanish, all sorrow will end,
And rulers will bow at your throne.
Our great commission complete,
Then face to face we shall meet

That sets a context for us and raises the question "Can a Nation be saved?" So back to Abraham who sees the need to appeal to God for clemency. He knows good and godly people, like his nephew Lot, lived in Sodom.

He cannot live with the thought that they may be destroyed along with the unrighteous and ungodly people whose lifestyle has become such an offence to God. After all Abraham has already had to save Lot and his family from the defeat of Sodom and Gomorrah by the king of Elam and others and knows that the area was spiritually and morally bankrupt. It is a place where children are left without security and stability in their lives, and, where no-one is safe from sexual perversion and attack. These are cities in a country where there is no accountability and people are driven by feelings and desires without regard for human dignity or worth.

Therefore this is the moment when Abraham has to speak out. God waits, He is ready to listen and respond.

God waits for Abraham's plea (v22). Abraham begins his petition with a question, or accurately, a challenge. "Will you sweep away the righteous with the wicked?" He follows that with the negotiating petition " What if there are fifty righteous people in the city? Will you sweep really it away and not spare the place for the sake of fifty righteous people in it? " (18:23-24) God has already affirmed Abraham as a man who will do what is just and right. God has seen Abraham's faith in action and credited it to him as righteousness (15:6) moreover God has demonstrated to Abraham His power to work miracles through the promise to make him a father of nations (15:4-5) and revealed to Abraham that nothing is too hard for Him (18:14). It is not surprising then that Abraham moves into faith filled, love fuelled intercession for those whose lives are righteous like his. Notice how Abraham takes his stand before the Lord (v22) and then approaches Him (v23) and then speaks. This is no casual or indifferent prayer, prayed as an afterthought or without getting 'up front and personal' with God. Abraham, through whom all nations will be blessed and whose people will be a powerful nation, has standing with God, because of a covenant relationship, because of faith, because of righteousness. He is prepared to risk God's anger (vv30 & 32), to speak with boldness (v27,31), and in humility (v27b) and to persevere until he gets to what he believes is a realistic position and to secure God's promise.

The result of this encounter is that Abraham, having laid himself bare, so to speak, before God in intercession, has to leave it with God. God has promised and cannot be unfaithful to Himself. The result is, as we know, that Lot and his daughters are saved and the cities of Sodom and Gomorrah are destroyed because of their sin. The stench of their unrighteousness has to be cleansed by fire.

I believe that we are in an Abraham moment for the church in the west. In the opening years of the new millennium, we have witnessed deceit and corruption in our governments, corporations and societies on a scale that have never been seen before. Morality is almost non-existent and there are few ethical standards that have any reference points in the will and law of God revealed in the life, teaching, death and resurrection of Jesus Christ. What is being exposed is just the tip of the iceberg. Whilst the media is having its day with lurid headlines and judgemental editorials, there is no repentance or integrity on the part of those who lead our nations or on the part of the people. Laws will not change the situation or restore truth. Only God can and he waits for his people to plead for their nation.

Will God find sufficient righteousness to forgive our nations? Will he lead the faithful to safety? Or will it be like Sodom and Gomorrah?

'Can a nation be saved?' Matt Redman picked up this question in 1996 when he wrote the song of which the first verse reads "Can a nation be changed?, Can a nation be saved? Can a nation be turned back to you?" The answer is in the chorus "We're on our knees, we're on our knees again, we're on our knees, we're on our knees again"

In the eighteenth century Wesley and the Moravians tilled the ground for world revival through continuous prayer. Indeed the Moravians interceded over a period of 100 years. Revival came through the Wesleys in England and America and through the Methodist missionaries in many parts of the world. Prayer brought about the Welsh Revival and then Azusa Street in America at the beginning of the twentieth century. In Indiana the Houses of Prayer movement saw more than three million registered converts as a result the intercession of one hundred thousand prayer cells.

The revivals in Argentina and Brazil were fuelled by prayer, so much so that Ed Silvoso wrote "When Christians begin to pray for the felt needs of the lost, God surprises them with almost immediate answers to prayer. In fact, prayer for the needs of that one-hundreth sheep is the spiritual equivalent of dialling 911. (That none should perish)

Scripture reveals to us how and why God would have us interecede.

- In 1 Peter 2:5 we are reminded that we are called to a priestly role of intercession.
- It is our duty to intercede, just as the Lord is making continuous intercession for us. Jesus told us a parable about a persistent widow and an unjust judge in order that we might learn that we must persevere in prayer (Luke 18:4b-8)
- The Apostle James, in his letter to the churches, reminds them that the prayers of righteous people avail much, even miracles of nature (James 5:16-18).
- God revealed to Solomon that in order for Him to forgive our sins and heal our land we must turn to him in prayer and repentance (2 Chronicles 7:14).
- All this is the work of the Spirit within us who intercedes through us, even when we do not know how to pray (Romans 8:26-27) and in whom we must pray at all times (Eph 6:18).

- The need for persistent prayer, at cost to us, is underlined by the prophet Isaiah who brought God's promise of restoration to Israel by reminding them of the need to speak out night and day and call on the Lord, giving themselves no rest. (Isaiah 62:1-7).

- God commands us also to take up the case of justice in Isaiah 59 and pray for integrity in the land. He sees the sin and unrighteousness and is appalled by it. God cries out for those who will plead the case for the land and seek light in the darkness.

- God speaks through the prophet Ezekiel and tells us to build up a hedge of protection around the country (Ezekiel 13:4-5).

I remember the Lord promising us (the intercessors) in one of my churches a few years ago that we would be known over a wide area and see people coming to the church who we never knew. We were so excited to be encouraged in this way. Over a short period of time we had people turning up at the church and meeting with God. Some people were converted in the car park as they sat in their cars wondering why they were there! Praying for people who we didn't know by name but knew of the darkness in their lives had a profound effect on them and us.

A few years ago when I was in Singapore on sabbatical I was attached to one of the larger Methodist Churches. It was here that I discovered the power of corporate prayer for the non Christian majority in the immediate area. The Methodist Church had set itself to 'Love Singapore' and their prayers and witness and community activities reaped a wonderful harvest and, I am sure, began a moral and spiritual renewal in that country. I visited churches of other denominations in Singapore also and found the same Spiritual fervour and intercession.

God raises the issue with us as He did with Abraham and waits for our response. A few years ago, whilst serving in my last circuit, God spoke to us about our area. This is called the Meon Valley circuit. It is situated in the county of Hampshire in Southern England. This is what was recorded in our circuit magazine.

I would firstly like to share with you the vision that we both had. The vision was in two parts. The first part concerned the circuits geographical extent. Angels lined the circuit from Hambledon to Wickham. They were waiting for a word to mobilise for revival. As the angels waited they unfurled a banner that stretched from side to side and over the whole circuit. As it unfurled the word "worship" could be clearly seen. At the far end a mighty wave of God's Spirit was poised to flood the circuit.

In the second part, God spoke to us about a 24 hour worship event to be called to "Release the River". As we prayed we felt that He was saying that we would need to have 12 banners in 6 pairs introduced during the worship — in some way these would signify the twelve tribes of Israel, but would also act as a call to the circuit to enter into a significant time of favour with the Lord. The banners would act as gateways through which the worship would progress and the circuit would move in prayer and praise ."

Many responded to this call and prayed and worshipped for this move of the Spirit in our area. Since February 2005 despite a small reduction in our numbers, we have seen over 100 new members received into our churches, nearly 41%increase in the small rural English circuit. I know that our response could have been much better, but we tried and God answered.

Chapter 6

"I will go" — Ananias (Acts 9:10-19)

"Faith and obedience are bound up in the same bundle He that obeys God, trusts God, and he that trusts God, obeys God "　　　　Charles H. Spurgeon

"When we walk with the Lord in the light of His word, What a glory he sheds on our way' While we do his good will, he abides with us still, and with all who will trust and obey: *Trust and obey, for there's no other way To be happy* in *Jesus, But to trust and obey."* John Henry Sammis (1846-1919)

When my sixteen year old son was dying of cancer his last two weeks were spent at home with the family. They were for us a time of growing together in love and our faith which were deeper than anything we had known before. It was a with a sense of anticipation that we greeted each new day. James slept downstairs in the lounge and we took it in turns to sleep on the settee near him. He awoke about 6.30am and although his eyes were badly affected by the growths both on his optic nerves and behind his eyes he would attempt to look out through the patio window and would shout to me "What's today dad?" Then we would pray together and he would pray for all his friends and for the family. He loved the Lord and he wanted to know what each special moment of the day would hold. This, in a way, the Lord's agenda. I know that these special memories of James have helped me to rejoice in my grief.

I cannot help thinking about James' morning greeting "What's today, dad?" It seems to me that this is the prayer of one who trusts and obeys. As Charles Spurgeon commented, trust and obedience are in the same bundle. I wonder if that bundle is labelled prayer? I think that in the case of Ananias it is. Here is one of the most. powerful examples of revival prayers that we could see. This type of prayer releases a Kingdom fruit which in mathematical terms is exponential. In other words it goes off the graph! Its effect is beyond our ability to determine. So I want to subtitle this type of prayer "**What's today, Dad?**"

This prayer has three parts to it. Firstly, there is the seeking prayer that I described in the introduction. Secondly there is the prayer of works through obedience and thirdly there is the prayer of impartation. The result is a miracle of healing and salvation as God's plan unfolds for the extension of His kingdom.

The seeking prayer

The "What's today prayer" is amazing. Be encouraged to really seek the Lord and wait upon Him Pray in the Spirit because this text [Acts 9:10-19] reveals that God really answers when you call. In Jeremiah 33:3 God promises to answer by showing us deep and unfathomable things. This certainly happened to Ananias. What could be more unfathomable than to be told that the arch enemy of the church had been set apart for the Lord's purposes? The manner of the communication is unfathomable too, especially for our Western, computer controlled, thinking. As Christians we can expect to hear from God in dreams and visions. Why? Because He said so! Joel prophesied that it would happen (Joel 2:28) and Peter, under the prophetic power of the Spirit at Pentecost, confirmed that the time had now arrived when this would be the experience of the believers until Jesus comes again(Acts 2: 17). In addition to this esoteric form of communication, God speaks so that we can hear. Ananias, a Spirit filled believer, had ears to hear. He knew the Master's voice (John 10:27) and he trusted what he was told because he was a child of God and knew the miracle-working power of God (John 10:28)

This prayer also teaches us about the awesomeness of God. When God directs us he does so accurately. When God gives us a word of knowledge, He is always right. When he says that it is a problem with the second smallest toe on the left foot that is precisely what it is. Ananias accepts what the Spirit says to him about the location of and direction to find Saul. He doesn't question the fact that the Spirit sees both himself and Saul simultaneously as they are praying or that the Spirit has just spoken to Saul also by means of a vision. It is a vision that is equally detailed and involves Ananias in a miraculous work viz. to lay hands on Saul for the restoration of his sight. Many times we can be in prayerful situations when we are given quite amazing insights into people's needs and can see where they can be found. On other occasions we may see danger for people and be led to pray very specific prayers for their help. Sometimes, in worship services and meetings we receive words of knowledge as to numbers of people with specific illnesses or in need of salvation. We may hear the Spirit tell us distinctly that certain people will receive healing, sometimes where they are seated or standing and sometimes through the laying on of hands or even by a word of command All in all God is entrusting us with divine knowledge and the promise of his word.

The seeking prayer is the key to God's will being done.

The prayer of works (obedience)

In the power of the Spirit, Ananias makes his way to where Saul is staying. It is an act of obedience and faith through which Ananias then shares in the glory of God. The Lord's brother, James, reminds us of this spiritual principle in chapter 2 verse l7 when he says that faith without works is dead.

Our response to our prayer is what brings life to others. This is important to understand If we were told during a telephone conversation that our neighbour's house was being robbed, would we just accept the information without taking action? No we would take appropriate action. So too it must be with what God tells us. Then, like Ananias, we shall see the kingdom waterfall of grace fall. We shall see the kingdom basket of gifts given and the glorious river of the Spirit begin to flow through someone's life touching many as it does. Saul is about to be filled to overflowing because of Ananias' obedience. What a privilege!

How important this prayer of works (Obedience) is in releasing others into their ministry. Since the day that Jesus walked in obedience to the cross, until He comes again, the power of the prayer of works, will go on releasing many millions into faith and ministry in all parts of the world.

The prayer of impartation

In our text we see that Saul is both healed and saved. He receives the baptism of repentance and a new man emerges, an apostle is commissioned. Ananias has to say the words to him as he lays hands upon him and God does the rest. This is not a petition to God but is a direct word from God to Saul. God makes good his word and Saul is used mightily of God. How many came to faith through Paul's preaching, his miracles and his teaching? We do not know exactly but Christianity spread from Jerusalem to Illyricum (Romans 15).

The prayer of works is no good without the prayer of faith, but together they work for the good of those who love the Lord. Imparting that faith in the power of the Spirit completes the prayer to the satisfaction of God. It might be all we ever do once in a lifetime but like Ananias the effect will be amazing.

I would like to conclude this chapter by sharing something that happened to me. Early in my ministry I was told by the Lord to pray for two people in the village where the manse/parsonage was situated. One was a young single mum who was into drugs and a permissive lifestyle. The other was a Jehovah's Witness with marriage and family problems, They were not my choice of people to pray for.

As I did pray for them over the next year the Lord gave me a real love for them both. Then one day, after visiting her a few times, he told me to invite the young mum onto an Alpha course. I did, she came. and ran away! Then the Lord confirmed separately to a lady in one of our Lydia groups exactly why the young mum had run away. She shared it with me and I knew that I had to go and see the young mum without delay. In her front room as I told her how much God loved her and that He had told us what she had just done, she broke down, completely in awe at God because no-one else knew what she had done, She gave her life to the Lord, repenting of her sins. She returned to complete an Alpha course and was completely changed. Her whole life is different. Her relationship with her son, who has become a Christian, is different as are her relationships with her mother and father. Her mother has become a Christian and this young mum is now a Methodist local preacher of some power! Her testimony has been published in full and has been on BBC Songs of Praise, Many have already become Christians through her ministry.

God led me on several occasions to the house of the Jehovah's Witness and built a relationship with him and his children. In times of great hardship God led us to Him at just the right time. He spent so much time at the manse that people thought that he had already become a Christian. Well, not yet. But watch this space! I must pray for him. Will I be his Ananias or will someone else? Only prayer will tell!

What I find inspiring about Ananias is that this is all that is recorded about him in the New Testament. A humble, prayerful man who is prepared to risk all in obedience to God, is used to change the life of Saul and release the Good News to millions. A one-time ministry? I think not, but it means that each one of us can be used by God to transform our nation and our community. We don't know how long Ananias had been on his knees before this moment of ministry to Saul, or indeed how long afterwards. It is easy for us in our consumer culture to expect immediate solutions and move on to the next thing. Ananias was faithful and persistent. His prayers really made a difference.

Charles Spurgeon commented on this attribute when he said, "by perseverance the snail reached the Ark".

Let us perfect the ability to get into the presence of God (Ps 46:10) and listen and then act. Pray the "What's today, dad" prayer and say "I will go".

Chapter 7

We'll walk the land — **Joshua**
(Joshua 1: 2-7)

If my people, who are called by my name, will humble themselves and pray and seek my face and turn from their wicked ways, then will I hear from heaven and will forgive their sin and will heal their land. (2 Chronicles 7:14)

We'll walk the land with hearts on fire; And every step will be a prayer. Hope is rising, new day dawning; Sound of singing fills the air. (Graham Kendrick – We'll Walk The Land verse 1 copyright Kingsway's ThankYou Music 1989)

[In one city, in response to a pastor's vision, several pastors prayed and fasted together for 21 days over two, five-gallon spray bottles filled with olive oil. Then, dressed in work clothes, they sprayed the ground around several of the most immoral establishments in their city, praying for God to intervene. Over the next year, over 50% of the places closed down." (Terry Tekyl – Blueprint for the House of Prayer)]

One of my first experiences of prayer walking the land took place in Cheshire, England. I had become the minister of a group of Methodist churches of which one was a small country chapel with no running water or toilets.

It had been built as a preaching place in a small village. Over the years the village had grown, having attracted families to work in the nearby towns. A ring road was built that gave it more accessibility and the dependence upon agriculture lessened, as more houses were built for office and factory workers. The village was made up of two groups. There were those who had lived there all their lives and then the 'incomers'.

Both Parish church and chapel had been there for many years. The chapel had a very small congregation, mainly those who had worked the land and lived locally for years.

Before I arrived to begin my ministry the Lord told me during prayer that I had to mission the village. When I arrived that is what I set out to do. I told the elderly congregation what He had said and an old couple wept. They said that they had been praying for revival in the village for thirty years and that someone would be sent who would spark revival. With a small team of Christians I set out a year long program of evangelism and witness, prayer and worship, involving the help of visiting speakers and a team from the Fellowship for Evangelization of Britain's Villages (FIBV).

The first thing that we did was to pray for the village and then we began to map the village and to prayer walk it. We stopped at key intersections and buildings and a place where a hanging had taken place centuries before and also a place where local legend said that a murder had been committed. Within days of beginning the prayer walking, a member of the local congregation rang me in a very agitated state to ask me to come quickly. When I got to the village she pointed out various animal and bird carcasses which had been hung from street lights and sign posts. Further investigation revealed that every street that we had walked had been visited by members of a local witches' coven and they had placed the carcasses to cancel out our prayers and curse the land.

I quickly discovered that the area had many covens and indeed the local warlock had pronounced his curse on us. As we prayed, more carcasses appeared until eventually the warlock was arrested (over other incidents reported in the local newspapers) and the witness in the village became more fruitful soon after.

At my other large church a few miles away, we faced a similar battle, when in the first move of renewal and a powerful anointing of the Spirit, another black witch coven in a nearby town, targeted a local farmer who owned a farm high up on the local hill, overlooking the town and church, and involved him in their rituals. He was talked into allowing them to use his farm to celebrate a summer solstice.

Providentially one of our Spirit-filled members, who had primarily visited the farm to see the farmer's wife, was contacted by him and he told her what was happening. He was very scared. They had told him that we had been targeted in their satanic rituals for downfall. High ranking Warlocks had come to the coven from other parts of England to oversee the plans and pronounce curses on the Christian community. The farmer was very vulnerable because his wife had died from cancer a year earlier and he was very lonely.

Needless to say that our intercessors got to work (we had many different groups at the time including our Timothy group for young people) and we prayer walked the farm, took authority in the name of Jesus and praised God. We even prayer walked the street in the nearby town where the coven met. It won't surprise you to know that the event they intended never took place! The farmer gave his life to Christ and became part of the Church, and God continued to move by His Spirit in our Church. The strategic importance of the hill could not be overlooked because the highest point of the hill was where, every Easter, we held a vigil from Good Friday to Easter Sunday, around a very large wooden cross that was bolted to secret fixings in the rock and wrapped in steel to prevent it being chopped down as it had been in previous years! It was high and holy ground claimed and used by the Church to declare the glory of God.

Everywhere that I have ministered I have encountered similar spiritual attacks, both on the church and myself. Everywhere I have prayer walked my 'parish' .

Why do I do this? The answer is because there is a spiritual principle involved. It is found in the book of Joshua in the first chapter. Joshua leads the wandering Israelites into the Promised Land with the promise of God ringing in his ears. God said to him

"Moses my servant is dead. Now then, you and all these people, get ready to cross the Jordan River into the land I am about to give to them—to the Israelites. I will give you every place where you set your foot, as I promised Moses. Your territory will extend from the desert to Lebanon, and from the great river, the Euphrates—all the Hittite country—to the Great Sea on the west. No one will be able to stand up against you all the days of your life. As I was with Moses, so I will be with you; I will never leave you nor forsake you. Be strong and courageous, because you will lead these people to inherit the land I swore to their forefathers to give them. Be strong and very courageous. Be careful to obey all the law my servant Moses gave you; do not turn from it to the right or to the left, that you may be successful wherever you go. (Joshua 1:2-7)

Sometimes we call this 'claiming the ground' but that is, I think, an unhelpful term. The decisive battle for our salvation has been won at Calvary. God has demonstrated His love for the world by sending His only Son to die for our salvation. He doesn't need to do it again.

It is said that for evil to triumph all that is needed is for good men to do nothing.

It is vitally important to grasp the need for the land to be cleansed/healed. That is why I have begun this chapter with the quotation from God's conversation with Solomon about repentance and forgiveness for both people and land. Land becomes infected by the sin of the people. It can become sterile and produce no crops. It can misbehave geologically and cause disasters. The land can become a hazard to health, breed infestations of poisonous and vicious insects and creatures. Wars, genocide, murder, political dictatorship, gangs, drugs, rape, torture all cause spiritual problems in and upon the land. Zimbabwe is a prime example of a country ravaged by inhumanity, genocide, dictatorship, greed, envy, occult practices, pagan religion and strife. There are many others, and one at a place near you!

Satan is the prince of this world (John 12:31; 14:30; 16:11). St Peter exhorts, *"Be self-controlled and alert. Your enemy the devil prowls around like a roaring lion looking for someone to devour. Resist him, standing firm in the faith, because you know that your brothers throughout the world are undergoing the same kind of sufferings."* (! Peter 5:8-9). Satan has gained access to us and the land through sin. He told Jesus that all the kingdoms of this world have been given to him. Jesus didn't deny that because it is true. The sin of Adam & Eve allowed Satan this dominion. In 1 John 5:19 we are told, *"We know that we are children of God, and that the whole world is under the control of the evil one"*. Only God can and will change all that when Jesus returns. In the meantime we need to raise our spiritual warfare to a new level.

The fact is that spiritual darkness, resulting from the presence of evil spirits will negatively affect the atmosphere and also hinder the activity of the Spirit of God in a building, or the land. There is also a general curse on the ground:

"Cursed is the ground because of you; through painful toil you will eat of it all the days of your life. It will produce thorns and thistles for you, and you will eat the plants of the field. By the sweat of your brow you will eat your food until you return to the ground, since from it you were taken; for dust you are and to dust you will return." (Genesis 3:17-19) This curse has been added to through the defilement of our sin: *"'Do not pollute the land where you are. Bloodshed pollutes the land, and atonement cannot be made for the land on which blood has been shed, except by the blood of the one who shed it. Do not defile the land where you live and where I dwell, for I, the LORD, dwell among the Israelites.'"* (Numbers 35:33-34).

We must prayer walk because our land and buildings are defiled because of murder, human sacrifice, abortion, sexual sin, idolatry and unclean animals. *"With a mighty voice he shouted: "Fallen! Fallen is Babylon the Great! She has become a home for demons and a haunt for every evil spirit, a haunt for every unclean and detestable bird."* (Revelation 18:2).

I believe, that unethical medical and scientific research including genetically modified crops and animals also defile the land. Isaiah brings the word of the Lord on this when he says " *The earth is defiled by its people; they have disobeyed the laws, violated the statutes and broken the everlasting covenant"* (Isaiah 24:5)

Surely ground is to be holy. God made it. Even after the fall, when calling Moses, God reminds him of this when he says *"you are standing on holy ground"* and later on when He said *"Put limits around the mountain and set it apart as holy."* *[Jacob at Bethel knew it because God 'was in that place]'* Walking the land in prayer and praise is a vital strategy for the kingdom. As we do so we will see breakthroughs in the lives of our own congregations, other churches and our communities. We must do battle so that we may occupy the land that is 'holy unto the Lord'. We will also see unity in the body of Christ and healthy people.

I still have a lot of prayer walking to do. I want to see a blanket of protection over the people and the area being filled with peace. I believe that as we mark our boundaries God's peace will break in to the life of our community. The receptivity level of non believers to the gospel will increase and the Lord will be glorified. Declining church attendance will be reversed. Sicknesses that seemed to prevail in an area will be overcome, gossip and slander will stop. Miracles will increase. We could begin to see an Acts 2:42-44 reality. God has promised, after all, that His glory will cover the earth as the waters cover the sea.

Joshua is perhaps one of the unsung heroes of the Old Testament. He was born in Egypt during the period of slavery and was a member of Ephraim, the tribe that was later at the heart of the Northern Kingdom of Israel. He was on the mountain where Moses received the Law. Joshua and Caleb, were the only spies sent out by Moses who were positive about the promised Land and entered it! Joshua was a leader, politically, spiritually and militarily.

The book of Joshua tells the story of a significant event, namely the conquest of the land of Canaan. The conquest of the land takes up the first twelve chapters and is instructive about how God's people are to enter the land that he gives them. The second part of the book, chapters thirteen to twenty two are about settling in the land. I think that it is important for us to understand that before we can "settle" the church we must first "conquer" the land.

Perhaps we need to hear too the admonition of the Lord with the same words that he spoke to Joshua "be strong and courageous". Put on the armour of God and let us pray in the Spirit for an open heaven.

There is a great song from Hillsongs, Australia. It is called "Touching heaven changing earth". May that be our goal as we walk the land and claim it as holy for the Lord.

PART TWO

Glimpses of Glory

Chapter 8
Memorials to God — **Cornelius**
(Acts10: 1-48)

"When Solomon finished praying, fire came down from heaven and consumed the burnt offering and the sacrifices, and the glory of the LORD filled the temple. The priests could not enter the temple of the LORD because the glory of the LORD filled it."(2 Chronicles 7:1-2)

"I will set a sign among them, and I will send some of those who survive to the nations—to Tarshish, to the Libyans and Lydians (famous as archers), to Tubal and Greece, and to the distant islands that have not heard of my fame or seen my glory. They will proclaim my glory among the nations. (Isaiah 66:19)

Δοξα: Doxa (Gk) – glory (as very apparent) in a wide application, literally, figuratively, objectively or subjectively; glorious, honour, praise, worship.

Kabod; (Hb) weight; but only figuratively, in a good sense, splendour or copiousness; gloriously, glory, honour (-able)

Philo, writing in *De Vita Mosis* describes the changed appearance of Moses on his descent from Mount Sinai. Philo states that, after forty days, "he (Moses) descended with a countenance far more beautiful than when he ascended, so that those who saw him were filled with awe and amazement; nor could their eyes continue to stand the dazzling brightness that flashed from him like the rays of the sun."[1]

Whilst the first two parts of Philo's statement follow the biblical narrative, the third seems to owe its origin to an oral or other written tradition. Nevertheless I like this. It seems very real and true to me and certainly accords with my experience. The glory of the Lord is not an illusory thing; it surely must be the reality of Him, present and active, transforming lives and His creation. Both the Hebrew and the Greek nouns describe both an objective and a subjective experience of God, that is awesome, weighty, glorious, beautiful, pure, powerful, supernatural, and, at times, like fire and consuming. God warned Moses that if Moses saw God's face he would die. On the other hand, St Paul likens the transforming work of the Spirit (2Cor 3:18) to the glory of God being seen/experienced in us.

I would have loved to be in Cornelius' house on the day that Peter arrived to preach the gospel, in response to Cornelius' request and the Angel's prompting. Peter's six Jewish Christian friends must have shared his awe at the sight and sound of The Holy Spirit transforming Cornelius and his household. Their faces must have been a picture! Their eyes full of light and their demeanour so changed.

Cornelius's "Memorials to God" were answered in a majestic and wonderful way. I take much encouragement and inspiration from this passage. I am less interested in the story of Cornelius as a second Pentecost, or a sign of the gospel being preached to the gentiles in Samaria, important though these are, but much more affected by the example of his prayer life. There can be no doubt that God's answer to Cornelius' prayers and witness, led to the gospel being taken by these new Christians far away from Samaria, Judea and Jerusalem, under the radar of the enemy, who would have been watching the apostles. I want to imagine other Roman soldiers in the Italian Regiment, saying to Cornelius and his devout batman soldier, 'what happened to you, you are so different', and being in awe of their 'glorious' appearance. I want to hear the friends and families of the servants and others present at this divine encounter, asking the same question and being in awe of the transformed appearance of the people before them. I rejoice at the witness of Peter and his fellow Jews as they tell James and the other apostles what had happened. Who knows where the news and the result of such a divine encounter travelled to accomplish the great commission?

What I have learned from meditating on this passage is that, in this instance, a God-fearing man and his household, are seeking to know God for themselves. They are attempting this through devout prayer (and fasting) and by caring for the poor. Whilst Cornelius had not become a Jew he worshipped the God of the Jews. He could not take his seat in the synagogue, because he was not regarded as a Jew, but he did follow the daily pattern of prayer. He was serious about knowing God and this showed in two ways, firstly his devotion to God in lifestyle and example, and secondly because he gave generously , in honour of God, to alleviate poverty and hardship in the lives of those Jews and gentiles who needed help. The result is that he is known to God by name. This is truly humbling for me as it reminds me that God hears the prayers of many, particularly those who are hungry for Him, and He hears prayers that may be prayed outside the 'church' and which are of a methodology which we have not 'taught'.

In verse 3, the Angel addresses him by name "Cornelius". I don't think that I have ever seen an angel, [and if I have yet not 'seen' then I ask God's forgiveness for my dullness]. However I know many people who have claimed to. A dear pastor friend of mine saw them all the time and spoke with them. He had a powerful prophetic ministry and we spent many times in wonderful prayer in the manse kitchen usually on the floor! When he and his congregation would come to our Methodist Church and join us for evening praise services, there was always an 'otherness' about our meetings and God always spoke and blessed us. Keith was loving and gentle in spirit, and a man after God's heart. He and his wife became very good friends and I preached many times at his meetings in Chester. Keith died very young, but his testimonies about angels certainly awoke something in me. People have told me that they have seen angels at my side during some Sunday services and during conferences. I have read many books where angels have played a significant role in God's plan for that person and their ministry. However, if I did see one and the angel spoke my name, I don't know what I would do....I wonder If would react like Cornelius, and stare at him in fear? His response is illuminating: 'what is it, Lord' he asked. I don't think that it was the Lord himself, although many times in scripture angels were used to describe God. I believe that this was an angel of The Lord, sent with a clear message to Cornelius. Luke makes it clear that this was NOT a vision but a real angelic being standing in front of Cornelius.

What is even more powerful is that the angel told Cornelius that God knew all about him! (shades of the story about the woman of Samaria). Furthermore that God not only knew but had heard Cornelius' prayers. They had come up to God as a memorial. The Greek μυεμοσυνον means a memorial, or something done to arouse the memory of another. F F Bruce says in his commentary on this passage that 'Cornelius's acts of piety and charity had ascended into the divine presence like incense or the smoke of sacrifice. God would honour the "memorial" with a suitable respons." This response, as we know is that Cornelius had to send for God's man, Simon (called Peter) who would tell him what he needed to hear and (by implication) reveal God's glory.

However, all this is not done in isolation, for like Ananias before him, Peter is some distance away (thirty miles) praying and having a supernatural encounter with God too. The result is, as I have already said, quite awesome and wonderful.

It reminds me of an experience some years ago. Within three months of my son's death at the age of sixteen, my walk with God had become much deeper. Out of the 'blue' my wife and I were asked if we would help another local Methodist Church, situated in a nearby village, to host a mission team. The church did not have sufficient members to work with the team or to host them. We prayed and felt a very strong push to say yes. The result was that for ten days we were involved in a remarkable mission that saw people converted to Christianity and others starting on the road to faith. Among this latter group were six boys, all teenagers with the exception of one, and all well known to the police! As I was, at the time, a youth leader and Sunday school teacher in my own church, I helped the team with youth events. The boys and I seemed to hit it off and after some initial behavioural problems our times together quickly became deep times of fellowship and honest sharing. Some of the team shared their testimony and the boys, being at the same school as my son had been, knew something about me. That led to some very deep and difficult questions being asked.

After the end of the mission, my wife and I continued to pray about these boys and felt led to open up our house to them each week so that we could build a youth fellowship. One evening the boys arrived and seated themselves in our large lounge, ready to learn some praise choruses and have teaching. Just then, a young lady, from one of our other churches, who had been a friend of our son, arrived and asked if she could join us. It quickly became apparent that she was not well and her constant coughing distracted the boys. I stopped the meeting and asked her if we could pray for her and ask the Lord to stop the coughing and heal her. I explained something of our healing ministry to the boys and asked them if they were comfortable for me to continue. They were and so the girl sat on a chair in the middle of the room, and my wife and I began to pray. We praised God and asked Him to presence Himself with us and reveal His glory. We then rebuked the cough in the name of Jesus and she immediately stopped coughing. We then laid hands upon her and prayed healing and wholeness for her. We had some word of knowledge about the nature of her 'sickness' and very quickly the power of God touched her and she was slain in the Spirit. There was a powerful and tangible sense of the presence of the Lord in the lounge. The boys were transfixed.

After a short time the eldest boy, who was actually very sensitive, got up. I asked him if he was feeling that he should pray for the girl and he nodded. I invited him to come round to the back of the chair where I was stood and then stretch out his hand over her, as a sign of his desire for her healing. As soon as he stepped within a foot of the chair he fell under the power of the Spirit. I caught him and let him down gently. I felt that he had walked into the glory of the Lord and been overcome by the weight of God's love and purity.

You can imagine by now that the other boys eyes were sticking out like chapel hat pegs! I gently explained what had happened to the older boy and asked them if they would like to ask Jesus into their lives. They all said yes and so I went round behind the chairs and settee where they were sat, and laid hands on them. As I did so they went out in the Spirit one by one. They looked like angels, it was quite amazing. I think now of Philo's description of Moses' face. They too were much changed in appearance from how they had arrived!

It was quite a sight! There was a holy silence in the room for over an hour! At 11.00pm my wife began to get quite anxious, worried that their mums and dads would wonder where they were. Soon they were in a fit state to go home. The girl stayed to share how the Lord had led her to us that evening because she needed ministry. The next morning, thankfully a Saturday, the boys were back complete with bibles found in their lofts or belonging to relatives, demanding an explanation of what had happened. They brought with them the youngest boy who had not been able to come the previous evening. Our fellowship with them continued for a number of years as they grew in the Lord and became a part of the church family.

More recently, I invited an anointed Chilean Pentecostal Methodist pastor to our circuit to preach. He stayed with me in the manse (Parsonage). The meetings were wonderful and God used my friend very powerfully. Most of our time together was spent in prayer and conversation about the Lord, as it is with so many of my friends who come to the UK to minister in our circuit. A telephone call from a church member resulted in a number of people arriving for an impromptu time of worship and praise (again not uncommon in my experience). The outcome of this, due to my friend's willingness to be obedient to God was that God met with us releasing some in tongues, healing others and generally transforming us in what an old Methodist Preacher used to call 'A Glory Time' It was a long night as many did carpet time whilst the Lord did what He wanted to do with them. Knowing them I can believe that God had heard their memorials and through the Chilean Pastor answered their prayers. They were all anointed for ministry and evangelism. Some have since accompanied me on ministry trips.

I believe that the Cornelius example is one to learn from today. Our culture and setting will be different. We know the Lord but He still desires to visit with us, bless, transform and equip. He wants fellowship with us, so that His transforming Spirit not only changes us but takes us on in our faith to share the gospel with others. St Paul says that we are to shine like stars in this crooked and depraved generation holding out the word of truth to them. (Philip 2: 15b-16a)

In this extract from Iris Ministries June 09 mission report, Heidi Baker writes:-
"On a Wednesday in May, after a deep and powerful time in our intimate prayer room, I felt the Lord lead me to minister to our staff from Ezekiel 47. As you may remember, the angel of the Lord led the prophet

Ezekiel deeper and deeper into the river. The Lord is leading us into the profound depths of His unending love. As we are immersed in His love, even in the most difficult times, things are still light, as if we're being lifted up and carried by the presence of His love. Ezekiel had to go beyond his comfort zone, into areas over his head, and it was in that place there were large numbers of fish. The Lord is longing for the lost to be brought in to His kingdom. They will be drawn to Him as we carry the freshness of His presence in the midst of the desert. Instead of working on our own with one little fishing pole, together we will pull the net and see a greater harvest. There will be supernatural fruitfulness flowing from His intimate love."

She then goes on to describe a mission trip undertaken in very difficult circumstances in which the weather is dreadful and their boats sink and they need to pay a lot of money for local fishermen to take them to their next village.

"The transfer from boat to boat was not easy, each craft being buffeted by waves, but through lots of prayer and careful manoeuvring we managed to accomplish it. The bottom of the canoe was filled with fish and fish slime and stank. I was excited now, thinking of Ezekiel 47. As our rescuers struggled to paddle through the rough sea, we were tipping heavily at times and really did not know if we would make it. The men, strong from years of fishing, pulled with all their strength to hoist the hand-made sail. Finally it was up and we caught the wind! If we will position ourselves in line with the Holy

Spirit, he will blow on us and we will get to our destination. As we started getting nearer to land, I shared the Gospel with the six Makua fishermen and they all accepted Jesus out there on the moonlit ocean. They had hauled in their catch, God had hauled in His. What a marvellous Holy Spirit theatre to share with the God who is relentless in pursuing His chosen ones into His kingdom. What a privilege it is for insignificant vessels of clay to be used in such a time as this, even with fears within and fears without."

(With acknowledgement to Iris Newsletters – Tenacious Love 7th June 2009)

There is a great lesson about unity too. We see a powerful picture of God, in Christ, uniting by His Spirit Jew and gentile, slave and free, male and female, God fearer and Born again Christian.

Let us pray to truly know God and to serve Him, let us seek to be in His transforming presence, so that His glory is revealed in us, increasing with each divine encounter so with Habakkuk we too can cry *"Lord, I have heard of Your fame; I stand in awe of Your deeds, O Lord. Renew them in our day, in our time make them known; in wrath remember mercy."* (3:2)

Chapter 9

Revive Your works, O Lord — **Habakkuk** (Hab 3:2)

The heavens declare the glory of God; (Psalm 19:1a)

Praise be to his glorious name forever; may the whole earth be filled with his glory. Amen and Amen. (Psalm 72:19)

For the earth will be filled with the knowledge of the glory of the LORD, as the waters cover the sea. (Habakkuk 2:14)

Prayer is the realization of the presence of God in our lives, the recognition of His presence with us, and our presence before Him. (Anon)

In the summer of 2008 we held a month long celebration in our circuit opening ourselves to the renewing power of God and seeking to go deeper with Him. The theme was "Glimpses of heaven". The vision for this came In November 2007 while I was in Slovakia for a European Methodist Prayer Conference. During the conference I felt God speak to me in my prayer time and say that he wanted me to host a time of refreshing in the circuit so that he could move us on to our next phase of mission. I asked a few of my co-speakers (who knew both me and the circuit very well) if they felt that this was 'of the Lord'. They did, and were also willing to come and help lead this time. They did and they said yes.

In early January 2008 I had a group of godly men booked to come in June and I told them that the theme would be 'Soar with the Spirit'. Then, while in a long prayer time early one morning, God spoke to me about the conference. He said quite audibly " you will call this time 'Glimpses of heaven' for I will show you things that you have never seen and heard before"! Needless to say that is what I did. We had an amazing time and God was true to His word. The conference was not without some backlash but the overriding response was of awe, joy and inspiration. Consider just one or two of the testimonies that came out of this time, bearing in mind that we have regularly seen the gifts of the Spirit at work, but never so much at one time. It was as if heaven was open and God was pouring out so many blessings (Malachi 4:10)

Here are some testimonies from that time:

On Wednesday we had house group and Scott (McDermott) came and we had a barbeque. Scott asked if anyone would like prayer. Well two or three us of stood up. I'd had trouble in the night with pain in my hip. It doesn't

bother me in the day but in the night the pain was so terrible it would cause me to shout out and wake myself up when I tried to turn over. I was prayed for and I had a brilliant night's sleep on Wednesday night and haven't had any pain since. Praise God.

Jean – church leader

I was one of the others that stood up with Jean at the barbeque for healing. I have to admit that I didn't feel any different on Thursday. It was a bad back. I have been a market gardener all my life until fifteen years ago when I went into the building trade. I have always praised God that I never suffered from a bad back despite all the bending. But recently I got a bad back. It has been really bad for the last two or three weeks. On Thursday at praise group practice Colin prayed for me and I haven't had any pain since and its perfect. *Dave*

I can't say that I have had a healing as such. When Scott arrived he told us that he didn't want to come as so much was happening in his church. I want to say that it is great that he came as some amazing things have happened here in the church since then. He prayed for me on Monday night and said some things over me that he couldn't have known other than from God. I have to say that I have felt different ever since he prayed for me. *Viv*

I can't claim being there on Wednesday but I was on Monday night and came forward when Scott was at the combined house group meeting. I just wanted to be blessed. At my age you have twinges of course, in your eighties you expect it. I went forward for healing. Scott discerned that I had a pain in my hand. I do suffer with pain in my hand. He was quite specific he said that three fingers were stiff. I was crying out in pain from my fingers and I went forward. Then he said that the wrist was painful too. I said yes it was like a pal of mine I've had it so long. But I haven't got it any more! *Joan – an elderly member*

It's not a healing for me but I've got a friend who I have known since I was eleven. I am Godmother to her three children. We were arranging a birthday party but she sent me a text to cancel and say that she was going into the cancer clinic. I rang her to see what was going on. I could tell she was really upset and she told me that they have found a lump in her breast so she had been fast tracked to the breast clinic. This took me by surprise as you hear about these things but never in people that you know. All I could say was that I would pray for her. So Graham (my husband) and I prayed and had the house group pray too. Our prayer was on the lines of "When she got to fast track clinic she would be all clear and there would be nothing". Last Thursday was the day and I waited all day to hear from her. At quarter past five she phoned to say that when she got to the fast track clinic there was nothing there. *Nicky*

I'm waiting for some physical healings but I have to say that the Lord has been healing on the inside. I think that they are some of the most amazing healings. You can't see them but you know that God is changing you. I had a vision the other night when Scott was here. It was so powerful. I've never felt the Holy Spirit presence like it before, it was so intense I just wanted to crawl up to Scott on my hands and knees and say we have to pray. I have never felt the Holy Spirit like this. During the meeting I had a vision of rows of angels above this place – blowing their trumpet. They are heralds saying Jesus the King is coming . Then I saw land: valleys and mountains, all green, and on the top of the mountains I saw the Lord with a red flag in is hand.

He was staking the flag onto the summit. Then I felt the holy spirit say that the land represented out lives. Jesus is coming to take back all those areas the enemy had claimed – all those high places and strongholds. He is coming to make is Kingdom manifest in our lives. His presence, His healing his kingdom is here. If you are one of those people like me who have been to many meetings and heard all the testimonies of healing and cried out like me 'when it is my turn' this is for you. I felt him saying that 'your turn is now'. His kingdom is here for you *Debbie*

I just really wanted to share how God transforms people. He's really transformed me in an amazing way. I was a Christian who liked to go out with his mates and have a drink and be 'Jack the Lad'. I have been sitting here and shaking, knowing that I have to get up and say that it all started about a month ago and I went to a meeting in Dudley. I was suffering from depression and being badly stalked. I am Ben but didn't know who I was. I got prayed for by an amazing guy. I went out in the Spirit and found myself somewhere and realised that it was heaven and it was so pure and I realised that I was at the feet of Jesus and I cried and cried. My tears were washing his feet and I could see the nail marks in his feet. Since then I have been asking what does this mean Lord and as time has passed I have sought to understand. After this weekend with these guys(in the circuit) I am back on track, I am so happy and I just want more of Jesus Christ in me. *Ben*

I was not happy when I heard that this conference had been organised. I did not want it. On Friday, however, God touched me in such a powerful way I know that it was the anointing of God. I also had a vision, a word, that sort of thing – a young man paddling up to his ankles at the seaside and the sea merged into heaven. The Lord was saying come deeper, come deeper. *Church Leader*

Well I have had verrucas for a couple of years and we have tried everything and I prayed and they went. *Joseph - young boy*

A third of his foot has been covered and it has stopped him swimming and playing sport. We have tried everything, creams, filing them, everything. Joseph dreamed that he was praying and asking Jesus to heal him. They just disappeared overnight. (Joseph's mum - latest testimony in July 2009 there is no sign of any verruccas.

Like the Apostle John who wrote that *Jesus did many more miraculous signs in the presence of his disciples, which are not recorded in this book.* (John 20:30) I can say something like that regarding the testimonies of what God did in giving us 'glimpses of heaven'. There are so many testimonies, more than we could record, but the real blessing is that lives have been significantly changed. I can see that faith levels have risen and there is a deeper hunger for the kingdom of God. It reminds me of God's response to Habbakuk 's complaint about the wicked when He said:

"Write down the revelation and make it plain on tablets so that a herald may run with it. For the revelation awaits an appointed time; it speaks of the end and will not prove false. Though it linger, wait for it; it will certainly come and will not delay. "See, he is puffed up; his desires are not upright— but the righteous will live by his faith— …….. For the earth will be filled with the knowledge of the glory of the LORD, as the waters cover

the sea……… But the LORD is in his holy temple; let all the earth be silent before him." (Habakkuk 2:2-4,14 &20)

I think that we entered the silent phase and we are still basking in the experience and the revelation of what God showed us. The result of all this is always a deeper longing for God and His kingdom. That is, I believe, what Habakkuk experienced and his response the God is very instructive from a prayer perspective. In Chapter 3 verse two, Habakkuk prays *"LORD, I have heard of your fame; I stand in awe of your deeds, O LORD. Renew them in our day, in our time make them known; in wrath remember mercy. "*

This is a prayer of praise and a proclamation of God's faithfulness, majesty and power. I believe that it is when, in remembering what God has done, the intercessor finds his or her spirit rising in faith and reaching up to heaven. It is a spiral of increasing fervency and expectation, for the spirit is reminded that God is forever the same and that nothing is impossible for Him. Habakkuk's prayer then moves him into the presence of God. He is leading us, today's intercessors, there too, to overcome and be in awe of His deeds. At that moment Habakkuk is ready to open his mouth to ask God for that which only God can do. He petitions God to renew His fame and His deeds despite the nation's unworthiness and sinfulness. He cries for salvation for the nation, the same cry that is on our lips in our time.

The whole book of Habakkuk is really a prayer - it is dialogue with God about the state of the nation, the threat of impending invasion by the Babylonians (1:6). It is a prayer prayed at a time of national emergency. The future of the nation and its' relationship with God is at stake. Habakkuk has no time to address oracles to Israel.

Habakkuk was known as a man of vigorous faith rooted deeply in the religious tradition of Israel and he is nothing, if not forthright, in expressing the feelings of the godly people in Judah. He seeks God, not with pious prayer or by blaming others for Judah's apostasy under the cruel Jehoiakim, but relying on God to save His people again. He accepts that God's ways are not man's ways and, having received God's reply, he responds with a beautiful song of faith: *"yet I will rejoice in the LORD, I will be joyful in God my Saviour. The Sovereign LORD is my strength; he makes my feet like the feet of a deer, he enables me to go on the heights. For the director of music. On my stringed instruments."* (3:18-19)

Habakkuk had a firm faith based upon the covenant promises of God. His joy and praise sprung from the relationship that God had with him and his people. Stripped of all else by the threat of the impending invasion, Habakkuk knows that he can never be deprived of his covenant with God. He can call God 'mine'. This intimacy of the relationship is sure and solid. He doesn't have to try and make anything happen to save Judah, instead he has to ask God to do it again. Like many intercessors since, Habakkuk has a strength and stamina to overcome fear and hardships and even to experience 'the heights'. *Those who trust in the Lord will renew their strength and rise up as on wings of eagles, they will run and not grow weary, they will walk and not grow faint* (Isaiah 40:31). Habakkuk begins in a depressed attitude but ends his prayer time with a sure confidence in God's provision and renewing power.

I have had to learn over the past few years to change my prayers for the nation to be more in line with Habakkuk. I found it too easy to approach God with a hit list of political leaders and parties, other nations, global companies, banks and bankers etc rather than to praise God and ask him to do again what he has done before. I have found the pain of my emotions tending to dry up my prayers and reduce my effectiveness. Since I began to follow this pattern used by Habakkuk I have found intercession much easier and more fulfilling. I am not advocating social irresponsibility by 'leaving it to God' and neglecting to speak out against injustice and tyranny, greed and hypocrisy. There are many things that cause me grave concern about our nation, the European Union and globalisation. There is great injustice in our society and the banking crisis, recession and unemployment bring additional challenges to both Christian and non Christian alike. As we turn to God in prayer and praise He turns his attention to us and His world.

We can be inspired by passages like Deuteronomy 33:26-29 as we pray like Habakkuk. What great heart we take from these words:

"There is no one like the God of Jeshurun, who rides on the heavens to help you and on the clouds in his majesty. The eternal God is your refuge, and underneath are the everlasting arms. He will drive out your enemy before you, saying, 'Destroy him!' So Israel will live in safety alone; Jacob's spring is secure in a land of grain and new wine, where the heavens drop dew. Blessed are you, O Israel! Who is like you, a people saved by the LORD? He is your shield and helper and your glorious sword. Your enemies will cower before you, and you will trample down their high places."

Equally we have the words of Jesus, which Habakkuk did not have. Jesus promises three times that he is coming soon (Revelation 22:7,12 and 20a) and he invites us to respond in the Spirit , *"come"* and *"Amen, come Lord Jesus"*

As we pray and love him obediently, God revives his works and His glory is revealed.

Here is a prophetic word given in June 2009 through one of our intercessors after hours of prayer asking God to move now. It was given along with the scripture from Deuteronomy 33:26-29 [above] AND Hebrews 10:37. I quote with permission from her written record of the world.

"Tell my people that I am coming again to remind them of my great love for them. [The feeling of His love for us was almost overwhelming and exceedingly great]. *I am coming in an unprecedented move to bring healing and restoration unlike any of you have ever seen and experienced. Those broken pots will be mended and all will be filled with My Glory* [I saw that the people were like big earthen pots. Those that were broken were put back together again and totally restored, and each pot filled with what looked like liquid gold and I knew it was the glory of God.] *to go from this place and take My light into the darkness – to illuminate all around them.* [I saw that as people when out into the darkness of the village, light emanated from them and lit up all around them, almost creating golden paths of light within the darkness] *Many will be attracted to the light of My Glory in this place.*

A well will be opened in this place. [It was a well that once opened would never dry up]

I have not forgotten you. Look up – see, I am coming even now"

Dutch Sheets tells a very interesting story in his book "Intercessory Prayer". He was scheduled to be part of a three day read-a-thon in which the whole bible was to be read from a position overlooking the capitol building in Washington DC. The read-a-thon followed immediately after a National Day of Prayer. The Lord had been speaking to Dutch Sheets during the prayer day about America. He says that he was due to read for 15 minutes maximum from wherever the previous reader had left off. He didn't know his reading time or the book from which he was to read. As he arrived he told the Lord 'Lord, there is only one way I could know of a certainty that You are confirming these things to me through my Bible reading. When I arrive they must tell me that I can read the book of Habakkuk or Haggai.' 'This was not a fleece, nor was I testing God', he says. 'It was because of the things that I had already sensed God was saying to me through these two books. Do you know the size of these books? They consist of eight pages in my Bible. What would the odds be, when not choosing my own reading – nor even the time of my reading, of my showing up and being told, "Here, read from these eight pages." I walked up to the lady in charge. " Are you Dutch Sheets?" "Yes, I am" "You are on in 15 minutes, after this person. You have your choice. You can either read the book of Haggai or the book of Habakkuk." I nearly passed out! You can believe I read the word of the Lord with authority, making prophetic declaration over the government of this nation with absolute faith that revival is coming."

O Lord, hear our cry. Come Lord Jesus, come. Let your glory cover the earth. Amen

Chapter 10
He's worth groaning for — **Paul**
(Romans 8:26-27)

For who among men knows the thoughts of a man except the man's spirit within him? In the same way no one knows the thoughts of God except the Spirit of God. We have not received the spirit of the world but the Spirit who is from God, that we may understand what God has freely given us. (1Corinthians 2:11-12)

The Spirit is the very life and power of God; all that he reveals is truth and power. He gives us to know God because he enters into the life and communicates the very thing which the word speaks in spirit and in truth. Through him we know God by what he is and gives and works in us. Thoughts can only give pictures of spiritual things. At times these may be beautiful and delightful pictures, which make most pleasing impressions. They may awaken strong desires in the heart and stir the will to itsb utmost effort, but they can never give or reveal the life. This is the sole prerogative of the Spirit of God. (Andrew Murray – *The Coming Revival*: Marshall Pickering)

"Sometimes I feel a burden of prayer; yet I may not know exactly what I should pray for; or I may not have exactly the right words to express what I feel. This is the time when I enter my spiritual language and can pierce through my natural inability to articulate to God what I am feeling." (Paul Y Cho - *Praye* : Word Ltd 1985)

"We never rise higher than our prayers. Since worshipping God is the main business of our lives, and prayer is the most intimate part of that, praying both identifies us and reveals our concept of God as nothing else can." (Frederick Pelser – *Prayer Made Practical* : Autumn House)

I read in a book of a newspaper headline in New York. It said "PRISON FOR HIS NOISY PRAYERS". The article went on to explain that Pastor Wilbur M Simmons had been sentenced to two months imprisonment at Macon, Georgia, for making too much noise whilst worshipping!

Sometimes our prayer times in church can be noisy affairs. We often have an open time of intercession when people are encouraged to lead us in prayer with spoken prayers that they feel God has placed upon their hearts. At other times we pray in small groups all at the same time and then the noise level can be quite high! Generally, it seems to me, our prayer times are very wordy and sometimes quite noisy. If it is very noisy then I find it hard to be still and say 'amen'. Prayers are perhaps too often temporal when they should be in the Spirit or spiritual (by which I mean of the Spirit). We are told in scripture that the pagans run after these things (Matthew 6:32). Some might think that I am instead advocating quieter praying. Not so! Quiet contemplative prayer is one way of praying but is not quite what I sense God is revealing to us in this passage of scripture from Paul's letter to the Romans.

The Holy Spirit is our teacher on how to pray and He is here leading us to groan! We should continually ask him to lead us, remembering that he is a God who seeks to live in us and fill us with truth, wisdom, power, love and the knowledge of Godhead. So, despite the possibility of imprisonment for making a noise, let us sigh and groan before God for revival!

There have been many occasions when I have had a burden to pray but not known precisely what to pray or why I am praying. This often occurs when God wakes me up in the early hours with a burden to pray. I usually go downstairs and wait on the Lord. Sometimes praise begins to erupt and situations or names come into my mind and my spirit begins to cry out to God. Other times there is a sense of weakness at the scale of a situation and I don't know how to pray. In these circumstances I have had the experience of some sort of 'tongue' but not my gift tongue, and I enter into His presence. Often it is not in any recognisable structure, instead there is a sense of, and this is the best way I can describe it, laying it before the Lord conscious that nothing is impossible for him. I have been silent, groaned, cried out, and grunted until I sensed an inner voice saying 'stop – that's enough'.

On many other occasions, particularly in meetings and worship, I will find myself, bowing repeatedly before God during intercession and groaning on the downward movement. Sometimes this is quite loud and a bit embarrassing. In some cases I have remained like this for up to half an hour before being able to stand up normally, in other cases I have fallen prostrate and continued to groan. Most of the time I have a sense of what is the focus of the grunting, but sometimes I don't. All I know is that God is doing something in and through me in prayer. There is, for me, a heavy anointing during these times. I call this type of prayer 'crunching' and I can say that it certainly tests the stomach muscles!!

I believe that when we position ourselves with the Spirit and are open and abandoned to the will and purpose of God, then two things happen. The first is that we become more aware of our own weakness in understanding and knowledge and the second is that God starts to take us to a place of travail which is his heart for the church, the people and the world. It is certainly wrapped up in a vision of life that is 'not yet' and glorious. Then it is tied up with the suffering that our poverty of spirit reveals. I think that the Psalmist David has it so right when he writes in Psalm 63:1-4

O God, you are my God, earnestly I seek you; my soul thirsts for you, my body longs for you, in a dry and weary land where there is no water.
I have seen you in the sanctuary and beheld your power and your glory.
Because your love is better than life, my lips will glorify you.
I will praise you as long as I live, and in your name I will lift up my hands.

And again in Psalm 42:1-2
As the deer pants for streams of water, so my soul pants for you, O God.

My soul thirsts for God, for the living God. When can I go and meet with God?

In the previous chapters we have looked at a variety of prayers which were spoken or sung. In this chapter we look at a quite different form of prayer that is no less powerful or relevant for today. This is the inexpressible prayer. It is Spirit prayer, Spirit intercession.

St Paul explains to the Church in Corinth the true purpose of the gifts of the Spirit and after setting these in the context of love, sets down some guidelines to help us understand the use and nature of these gifts. One of the gifts is that of "tongues". St Paul claims to speak in tongues more than anyone else at the time (1 Corinthians 14:18) but he emphasises that when he does his mind is unfruitful (1 Corinthians 14: 14). When he speaks of love he does so making clear that whether we speak in the language of men or of angels, our language is just noise, if there is no love behind it (1 Corinthians 13:1). Equally St Paul makes the important distinction between tongues and human speech, by saying that anyone who speaks in tongues does not speak to men but to God. Indeed, he says, no one understands him; he utters mysteries with his spirit….(1Corinthians 14:2). Praying in tongues then is both spiritual and powerful. This suggests to me that it is a very important weapon in the mouths of the church. It is a weapon of our warfare and has divine power to demolish strongholds (2 Corinthians 10:4). So if praying in tongues is so powerful how much more would Spirit prayed prayers be?

I read this description of tongues in David Pytches' book 'Come Holy Spirit'. He quotes from an article written in the Renewal Magazine in 1984 by Rosemary Attlee. She wrote, *"How can I describe this heart language of the Spirit, but as a love language for the Father's ear? An intimate language springing to the lips in times of pain, grief and fear, as well as joy...it is not only a superb piece of practical equipment, but in its use there seems to be a pervasive and wholesome aroma of the Holy Spirit, a fragrance my spirit breathes in".*

Sighs and groans, it seems to me, in the context of Romans 8:26-27, may fall in to the category of tongues that do not need an interpretation or cannot be interpreted. Perhaps they are intended to be used only in private or open intercession. The test of such 'tongues' edifying the church or leading to the conversion of unbelievers is obviously harder to apply than with tongues that have an interpretation or where the hearer understands directly by the Spirit.

Professor Gordon Fee, in his great book on the Holy Spirit entitled *"God's empowering Presence",* rightly makes the point that to understand what our 'weaknesses' are we need to understand what the adverb 'likewise' means at the beginning of the sentence in verse 26. He reasons that this verse is linked, neither to verses 24-25 nor to verse 23 but to verse 16. Therefore it is the work of the Holy Spirit to bear witness with our own spirits (summarturei = summarturei which means to show to be true or to give evidence in support of) and to assist us in our weaknesses (sunantilambanetai = sunantilambanetai which is from the root verb meaning to help or join with). In this way the work of the Spirit is helping us to endure with patience (v25). This we do, in the understanding of St Paul, because we already live in the 'not yet'. We participate in present suffering for future glory. However the most interesting and controversial aspect of this 'tongue' is that it is not expressed in words. The Greek alaletos = alaletos in verse 26 means just that. I like the idea that this prayer may be inexpressible i.e. without any words to use or inarticulate in other words where it is too deep for words.

Some commentators have come to the conclusion that this type of prayer is silent. In any event this is 'praying in the Spirit' (1Corinthians 14:14-15 and Ephesians 6:18) in which case the Spirit is interceding for us even though we don't know what we are praying for. I think that this is because God's Spirit searches our hearts and knows our thoughts and desires (Jeremiah 17:10; Acts 15:8 and 1 Thessalonians 2:4). When these are within God's will and point to a future glory then the Spirit can bear witness to God about us and bring before Him our heart's desire. This type of prayer is quite awesome when we understand that the Spirit prays within the believer and He does so with words which are not understood by the person praying! I relate this to the Spirit crying with my spirit 'Abba, Father' (Galatians 4:6) and far from being passive in this prayer we participate with the Spirit by being open to Him and having God's will in our hearts. Thus God cannot do anything other than to answer.

I loved the story about George Muller involving a prayer for help at a time when there was no breakfast for the orphans at his Ashley Downs orphanage. A small girl whose father was a close friend of Muller was visiting in the home. Muller took her hand and said, "Come and see what our Father will do." In the dining room, long tables were set with empty plates and empty mugs. Not only was there no food in the kitchen, but there was no money in the childrens home account.

Muller prayed, "Dear Father, we thank Thee for what Thou art going to give us to eat." Immediately, they heard a knock at the door. When they opened it, there stood the local baker. "Mr. Muller," he said, "I couldn't sleep last night. Somehow I felt you had no bread for breakfast, so I got up at 2 o'clock and baked fresh bread. Here it is." Muller thanked him and gave praise to God. The Spirit took what was on Muller's heart and brought George Muller and his heart's desire before God, who answered instantly, in fact, before George Muller asked.

Soon, a second knock was heard. It was the milkman. His cart had broken down in front of the orphanage. He said he would like to give the children the milk so he could empty the cart and repair it.

God has called us and equipped us to pray and have intimacy and fellowship with him. He has given us all we need through Jesus Christ who is our life and he is with us by his Spirit. But there are times when life is just simply too big, and too complex, and *we do not know what to ask for*. In such times, we know neither what to pray for, nor how to present our petitions, as we ought. This is when the Holy Spirit intercedes on our behalf. How gracious is He, to share with us the bearing of this burden.

In Psalm 119:148 we read: *My eyes stay open through the watches of the night, that I may meditate on your promises.*

I am reminded again of the devastating floods in Mozambique in January 2008. Not many countries in our modern world have been hit by disaster so often. Rolland Baker wrote the following about their reliance on God at that critical time: "Already one of the poorest countries of the world, it struggles without the mechanisms of modern countries that can deal to a great extent with regional weather fluctuations, food shortages and medical emergencies. Its transportation infrastructure barely exists. There is hardly any safety net for the poor. Much of the world suffers from "compassion fatigue," and well-known relief agencies in Mozambique struggle with funding and distribution challenges. Christians hardly know what to do with still more pleas for financial help. We are all tempted to run and hide, and try to find some protection from all the assaults on our peace in this world. Forces of evil seem to get away with so much.

But we are not helpless, and even in our weakness we find strength. We have a source of never-ending goodness and energy. This source is not impersonal and remote, unlikely and sporadic. No, this source is a personal and perfect Saviour, the only person who can make sense of our lives in this world. He makes Himself available to all who call upon Him. And to those "who by persistence in doing good seek glory, honour and immortality, he will give eternal life" (Rom. 2:7).

Rather than seeing discouragement on all sides, we preach power and total salvation in every circumstance. Every disaster leads us to lean on our Saviour all the more, and to depend on Him alone. Our joy is to be able to encourage believers everywhere even while facing the most overwhelming damage done by the enemy. In such situations, we cannot afford to be doubtful and down, depressed and immobile. No, in every circumstance we are called to be "more than conquerors through him who loved us" (Rom. 8:37). If we look into His eyes, there will always be enough, because He died!" "

What an amazing testimony and sharing in God's heart! Whilst there is real suffering among the people continually caught up in man made or natural disasters there is a deeper pain for Heidi, Rolland and their team as they know what God has in mind for his people. This is where, for me, sighs and groans too deep become the power of salvation and revival. It is interesting to note that Rolland commented in his article on how the church always grows during these disasters!

Lord, the cry of my heart is for your kingdom to come and your will to be done. I cry for the lost to know salvation and for your righteousness, peace and joy to be our experience as your children. Amen, Amen, hallelujah our God reigns!

CONCLUSION

I hope that, if nothing else, this book will have inspired you to seek God in prayer for the lost and unsaved, and especially, the Church. I hope that God may use you like Ananias for the strategic purposes of releasing someone else into powerful kingdom service or like Elijah to change the nations. I pray that He will press some of you into action like Nehemiah or give you a new prayer tongue, more powerful and effective than you have known before.

It seems to me that time is short and God is calling the Church to learn how to release the fragrance of incense in prayer. He wants the unsaved to be saved, He wants to ravish our hearts with His love. He desires intimacy with His creation. What He has laid before us is not a mechanical act or a religious rite but the incredible privilege of building our relationship with Him in prayer, through which He will open our eyes to the far horizons of His kingdom. For me intercession is revelatory, the Spirit delights to live in our worship, praise and prayer, releasing understanding and wisdom, power and authority. What no eye has seen and no ear has heard and what no mind can conceived, he wants to make known to us as we pray His word into being.

There is such an eschatological purpose to this too. The two kingdoms are at war. The kingdom of this world ruled over by Satan versus the kingdom of God ruled over by Jesus. The only true and lasting reality is the kingdom of God and of heaven. Prayer helps us to keep in the kingdom of God whilst revealing it to the world as heaven touches earth in answer to prayer.

For many years I have been aware of the spiritual battle being fought for our lives. On the one hand there is the inexorable move to globalization, one world government and religion and on the other hand there is Christianity, not the religion, but the true body of Christ, Spirit filled and led, standing firm for truth and justice, love and peace. The one acts immorally and unethically with lies and deception and unelected groups in charge, the other in righteousness and truth. One sounds good and plausible the other really is. The one is bound for death and hell, the other for eternal life.

If every good, righteous, faithful and joyful aspect of life were like books on a shelf (which the Holy Scripture is), then prayer is the book ends that keep it all as one. Without the support of the book ends the books are easily disturbed and can become dislodged. The remorseless attack on family, marriage, faith and personal liberty represent an ever present threat to the stability of society.

Let us become prayer warriors, interceding with persevering, passionate prayer, so that His kingdom comes and His will is done on earth. Let the Spirit lay on your heart the prayer burden from the throne room so you can pursue that until He says stop or lays another burden on your heart.

Appendices

The Upper Room — Rev Dr Rob Frost, *Share Jesus International*

Live Worship (dvd) — Terry McAlmon, *TMMI*

The Sound of Heaven (dvd) — Terry McAlmon, *TMMI*

Pray the Price — Terry Teykle, *Prayer Point Press*

Blueprint for the House of Prayer — Terry Teykle, *Prayer Point Press*

If my people (dvd) — The Methodist Church, *Ignite Revival Network*

Let the sea resound — The Sentinel Group, *Gateway Christian Media*

Transformation (videos) — The Sentinel Group, *Gateway Christian Media*

Bibliography

The Biography of Robert Murray McCheyne	Bonar, Andrew *Marshall Pickering*
Vision at Patmos	Catherine & Justo Gonzalez *Abingdon*
'Catch the Fire' The Toronto Blessing	Chevreau, Guy *Marshall Pickering*
Pray with Fire	Chevreau, Guy *Marshall Pickering*
The Lost Art of Intercession	Goll, Jim W. *Revival Press*
God on Mute	Greig, Pete *Survivor*
Red Moon Rising	Greig, Pete and Roberts, Dave *Survivor*
Effective Fervent Prayer	Isleib, Mary Alice *Ministries*
Watch and Pray	Lambert, Lance *Kingsway*
The Message of Revelation	Wilcocks, Michael *BST*
The Coming Revival	Murray, Andrew *Marshall Pickering*
The Coming Christ	Murray, Andrew *Marshall Pickering*

The Church Invisible	Page, Nick
	Zondervan
Prayer made Practical	Pelser, Frederick
	Autumn House
That none should Perish	Silvoso, Ed
	Regal
Intercessory Prayer	Sheets, Dutch
	Regal
Spiritual Power	Sherwood Elliot Wirt
	Lion Books

What on earth are we doing to our children
　　　　　Maranatha Community, *Maranatha*

The Three Battlegrounds	Frangspaie, Francis
	Arrow Publications
Evangelise Spirituality	Gordon, James M.
	SPCK
Come Holy Spirit	Pytches, David
	Hodder & Stoughton
God's Empowering Presence	Fee, Gordon
	Eerdmans